POCKET IMAGES

Darlington

POCKET IMAGES

Darlington

George Flynn

NONSUCH

First published 1992
This new pocket edition 2007
Images unchanged from first edition

Nonsuch Publishing
Cirencester Road, Chalford
Stroud, Gloucestershire, GL6 8PE
www.nonsuch-publishing.com

Nonsuch Publishing is an imprint of NPI Media Group

British Library Cataloguing in Publication Data.
A catalogue record for this book is available from the British Library.

ISBN 978-1-84588-413-0

Typesetting and origination by NPI Media Group
Printed in Great Britain

Contents

Introduction

The prince-bishops of Durham, who were lords of the manor of Darlington, had vice-regal powers, including the right to levy taxes and to grant market charters. Towards the end of the twelfth century Darlington was raised to the status of one of the bishop's boroughs with the right to hold markets. The borough, centred on the market-place, was bounded on the east by the Skerne, on the south roughly by the line of Beaumont Street, on the west by a line to the rear of Skinnergate, and on the north by an irregular line which ran to the south of Bondgate then northwards to encompass part of Northgate before turning east again to return to the Skerne. Within these boundaries the borough's freeholders lived, paying a money rent to the bishop. Within the separate manor of Bondgate lived the bishop's customary tenants who were required to supply goods or perform services for the lord of the manor such as transporting fish and wood, repairing fences or mowing hay. Customary tenancies could not be transferred automatically to sons and heirs or handed on directly to another tenant without the consent of the bishop or his officials and the payment of an entry fine. Technically the tenancy was surrendered into the hands of the lord of the manor and then regranted. In time the duty to perform services was commuted to a money payment and the transfer of property became a legal formality under copyhold tenure until its abolition in 1926.

To safeguard his interests the bishop appointed a Borough Bailiff who presided over the Borough Court. From the seventeenth century the post was often held by a lawyer, and by the middle of the nineteenth century the duties of the bailiff had become largely honorary, although he was still considered to be the chief citizen of the town. The office was officially abolished in 1867.

In 1850, as a result of the Public Health Act of 1848 and a National Board of Health investigation into the sanitary conditions of the town, a local Board of Health was established, the first elected body to govern Darlington. Further pressure from the townspeople resulted in an enquiry conducted by a Parliamentary Commissioner and, in 1867, Darlington was granted municipal borough status with the right to elect a mayor and eighteen councillors. With ever increasing boundaries Darlington became a County Borough in 1915, but under the Local Government reorganization of 1974 was reduced to the status of a non-metropolitan district. The Queen, however, granted a charter to the town which permitted the retention of its borough status with the attendant right of having a mayor as its chief citizen.

Unlike other counties, Durham did not send two members (knights of the shire) to represent its interests in Parliament as it was considered that the bishop was the county's representative in the House of Lords. It was not until the seventeenth century, when the county had its own MP during the Commonwealth period, that Durham was represented in the House of Commons. With the restoration of the monarchy and the re-establishment of the bishopric, Durham was again disenfranchised but, in 1673, regained the right to return a member to Parliament. After the Reform Act of 1832, the county returned four members, two each for the northern and southern divisions. In December of that year Joseph Pease of Darlington was elected as one of the MPs for the southern division, the first member of the Society of Friends to be admitted to Parliament. In 1841 he was succeeded by his brother, Henry. In 1867, as well as acquiring municipal borough status, Darlington became a Parliamentary borough with the right to return its own MP and Edmund Backhouse (Liberal) was duly elected. To date thirty-six elections have provided the town with fifteen different MPs: five Labour, three Liberal, two Liberal Unionists and five Conservatives.

Darlington's prosperity in the medieval period rested mainly on its status as a market town dealing in livestock and wool, and on the production of woollen cloth. The bishop received rent for both a fulling mill and a dyehouse. From the late seventeenth century Darlington became famous for its production of linen, particularly of a type of cloth known as huckaback, woven in widths which could be found nowhere else in the country. It was the textile industry which brought representatives of both the Pease and Backhouse families, whose descendants were to play such important roles in the later development of the town, to Darlington. Joseph Pease built the first worsted mill in the town in 1752.

There is also considerable evidence to show that the town possessed a substantial tanning and leather industry from medieval times, no doubt an offshoot of its cattle trade. At the beginning of the nineteenth century the town claimed that it produced more leather than any other comparably sized town in England.

Until the construction of the A1(M) bypass Darlington lay on the main east coast route from the south to the north and Scotland, serving as a major coaching and posting stop where horses were changed and passengers were provided with accommodation and refreshment. As a result the town and its inhabitants have received mention (not always complimentary) in official despatches, journals and diaries.

Darlington's transformation from a relatively small, compact market and textile-producing town to a major industrial centre was largely the result of the foresight of Edward Pease who, at the beginning of the nineteenth century, invested his time, energy and wealth in persuading his fellow townspeople to accept a new-fangled method of transporting coal from the west Durham coalfield. It was Pease who invited George Stephenson to visit the town to advise on the feasibility of building a railway from West Auckland to Stockton and to become its first engineer, and who later supported Stephenson by persuading a doubtful committee (and Parliament) that steam locomotives should be used to haul the trains.

With the advent of the railway the demand for iron and steel resulted in the establishment of small foundries which, over the years, developed into large iron and engineering companies producing pressure vessels, bridges and large components for ships, as well as products for the railway industry.

With heavy industry now in decline Darlington's engineering base has been drastically eroded, but the town's communications by road, rail and air and its pool of skilled labour have encouraged the establishment of light, service and high technology industries.

Darlington's industrial expansion in the nineteenth century resulted in a rapid increase in the population and a subsequent demand for housing. The small houses which had been built in the yards leading off the town's main streets became subject to multi-occupation and increasing overcrowding. Some of the houses built in the areas of Bank Top, Parkgate and Albert Hill were not always well constructed, adequately drained or supplied with mains water. A health report of 1850 highlights some of the atrocious conditions but, gradually, successive energetic Medical Officers of Health produced reports which resulted in steady improvements to the townspeople's living conditions and quality of life.

Those who could afford to do so built spacious houses and villas outside the town centre to gain the advantages of gardens and clean air. While many of these houses have subsequently been demolished, others have survived, although converted to other purposes and marooned in a sea of later development. In some instances remnants of these former estates survive as public open spaces.

While the wealthy Quaker families of the town were sometimes criticized for building these minor 'stately homes', it should not be forgotten that they contributed freely to a multitude of philanthropic causes in the town, particularly those connected with health and education.

As with so many other towns and cities, some of Darlington's post-war redevelopment has been unfortunate although, thankfully, not as drastic. The re-siting of the market-place and the demolition of the market hall and town clock were only halted at the eleventh hour. Overall, the Cornmill shopping centre has been successful, although retail tenants come and go and there are always empty units. The problem of the volume of the traffic on all approach roads to the town centre has still to be solved. The Pedestrian Heart project (officially opened in June 2007) which has involved the drastic rerouting of bus services and the redesign and urban landscaping of High Row, Prebend Row, West Row, Blackwellgate and part of Northgate caused much controversy, not to mention disruption and loss of trade for many businesses The impact of the proposed Oval development on the site of the Commercial Street car park (due to open in 2010) remains to be seen.

Communities are living entities, continually in a state of flux. It would not be reasonable to expect that buildings will last for ever and townscapes will never change but vigilance is still necessary to prevent the needless destruction of our heritage. Economic necessity and the overriding profit motive which seems to rule the life of the nation must not be allowed to sweep away those parts of our heritage which cannot be seen to 'pay their way'. Sensitive redevelopment of existing buildings, for example the Lingfield Point business units in the former Paton & Baldwins offices and ballroom (see p. 117), has been highly praised but the decision to build part of the Eastern Corridor by-pass over part of the track bed of the 1825 Stockton and Darlington Railway is to be regretted.

One

Darlington

A standard postcard with a background of 'beauties'. The publishers adapted the design to produce cards for many different towns and cities.

A COPY OF THE

Charter of Incorporation

OF THE

BOROUGH OF DARLINGTON,

GRANTED BY HER MOST GRACIOUS MAJESTY,
QUEEN VICTORIA, ON THE 13TH DAY
OF SEPTEMBER, 1867.

DARLINGTON:
PRINTED BY WILLIAM DRESSER, HIGH ROW.

1867.

THE

CHARTER OF INCORPORATION.

VICTORIA, by the grace of God of the United Kingdom of Great Britain and Ireland Queen, Defender of the Faith, To ALL TO WHOM these presents shall come greeting:

WHEREAS, by an Act passed in the First year of our reign, intituled "An Act to amend an Act for the Regulation of Municipal Corporations in England and Wales," it was enacted, that if the inhabitant householders of any town or borough in England or Wales should petition us to grant to them a Charter of Incorporation, it should be lawful for us by any such Charter, if we should think fit by the advice of our Privy Council to grant the same, to extend to the inhabitants of any such town or borough within the district to be set forth in such Charter all the powers and provisions of an Act passed in the Session of Parliament held in the Fifth and Sixth years of the reign of his late Majesty King William the Fourth, intituled "An Act to provide for the Regulation of Municipal Corporations in England and Wales," whether such town or borough should or should not be a corporate town or borough, or should or should not be named in either of the Schedules to the said Act to provide for the regulation of Municipal Corporations in

From September 1850 Darlington was governed by a Board of Health, elected by property owners and occupiers in the town. In 1867, following a petition from the townspeople, a Charter of Incorporation was granted by Queen Victoria. From then on Darlington was to be governed by a mayor, aldermen and councillors. The franchise was restricted to males who occupied, resided and paid rates for a house, warehouse, counting-house or shop. The original charter is kept in the Town Hall.

PROCLAMATION.

Be it known to you, O Men of the North, that the battle between the People and the Forces of Reaction starts at 8 o'clock this morning.

See to it that there are no laggards on the People's side.

Then Victory will be yours.

God Save the People!

PUT IT THERE

LINCOLN	X
PEASE	

THE BALLOT IS ABSOLUTELY SECRET

Ignatius Timotheus Trebitsch Lincoln, born April 1879 in Hungary, became a British citizen in May 1909, one month after he was accepted by the Darlington Liberal party as a candidate for the January 1910 General Election. Trebitsch Lincoln defeated the sitting MP, Herbert Pike Pease, by a majority of twenty-nine. In the next election, held in the December of the same year, Trebitsch Lincoln did not stand and Pike Pease regained his seat. Subsequently, Trebitsch Lincoln was claimed to be a German spy and, after a spell in jail, was deprived of his British citizenship. He ended his varied colourful career by becoming a Buddhist abbot in China.

JONATHAN MARTIN
THE LUNATIC,
Who set York Minster on Fire, February 2, 1829.
From a Painting by Mr. E. Lindley, taken in Prison, by permission of the Magistrates.
YORK :—Published by H. BELLERBY, 13, Stonegate.
March 31, 1829.

Jonathan Martin, a Northumberland man, was press-ganged into the Royal Navy during the Napoleonic Wars. After his discharge he worked for a time in Darlington. On 1 February 1829, after attending evensong in York Minster, he hid himself in the building and subsequently set fire to cushions and prayer books.

THIRD EDITION, CONSIDERABLY IMPROVED, WITH ENGRAVINGS BY THE AUTHOR.

THE

LIFE

OF

JONATHAN MARTIN,

OF DARLINGTON, TANNER,

WRITTEN BY HIMSELF,

CONTAINING

An Account of the Extraordinary Interpositions of Divine Providence on his behalf, during a period of six years service in the Navy, including his wonderful escapes in the Action of Copenhagen, and in many affairs on the coasts of Spain and Portugal, in Egypt, &c. Also an account of the Embarkation of the British Army after the Battle of Corruña. Likewise an account of his subsequent Conversion and Christian Experience, with Persecutions he suffered for Conscience' sake, being locked up in an asylum and ironed, describing his Miraculous Escape through the Roof of the House, having first ground off his Fetters with a sandy Stone. His singular Dreams of the Destruction of London, and the Host of Armed Men overrunning England, also of the Son of Buonaparte taking England, &c. &c.

Mark! my kind readers, the hand of God in a poor humble cot, God has raised of us four brothers; my oldest brother he has made a Natural Philosopher, my youngest, an Historical Painter, his drawings and engravings has made Kings and Emperors to wonder. The Emperor of Russia at this time has made him a present of a diamond ring, but I, the unworthiest God has given to me the gift of prophecy, which is the best of all, for I feel that God is with me.

Lincoln:

PRINTED FOR AND SOLD BY THE AUTHOR BY R. E. LEARY, 1828.

Price Sixpence.

The resulting fire destroyed the organ and the choir roof and stalls. A description of Martin, who was well known in York, was circulated. He was eventually arrested in Hexham in possession of incriminating evidence. At his trial he was found guilty but insane and was committed to a London asylum where he died nine years later.

The outbreak of war in August 1914 saw the rapid mobilization of many Territorial units. Darlington, a major railway junction, was an ideal assembly point. Public parks and private parklands were commandeered and turned into military camps. The Northumbrian Brigade of the Royal Field Artillery (Territorials) gathered in South Park, before crossing to the Continent to fight the enemy.

The 4th Battalion of the Yorkshire Regiment (Territorials) was assembled in the extensive grounds of Hummersknott (the former home of Arthur Pease). Here a drum and fife band leads a detachment into the tented camp.

The county's own Territorial battalion, the 5th Durham Light Infantry, was also based at Hummersknott (now part of Carmel Comprehensive School). The soldiers in this photograph are marching with their rifles 'at the trail'.

In 1939, despite the general feeling that 'the war would be over by Christmas', instructions on what to do in the event of an air raid were issued. More than fifty years on, the wail of an air-raid siren still has the power to send cold shivers down the backs of those who are old enough to remember the Second World War.

AIR RAIDS

The public of Darlington should be clear as to the procedure with regard to Air Raids.

1. There are **9 Air Raid Sirens** geographically situated so that the whole of the town is covered.

2. If **HOSTILE AEROPLANES'** are known to be approaching **THIS AREA** these sirens will sound a **WARBLING NOTE** (that is to say, a blast alternately rising and falling in pitch) for **TWO MINUTES.**

3. Every person should immediately **GET OFF THE STREETS** and make for **HOME** or the **NEAREST SHELTER.**

4. As soon as it is known that the **HOSTILE AERO-PLANES HAVE PASSED** the sirens will again be sounded for two minutes. This time they will give a **CONTINUOUS BLAST** at a steady pitch.

5. **THIS DOES NOT NECESSARILY MEAN THAT THE DANGER IS OVER,** as the enemy may have dropped gas bombs, or gas in spray form.

6. Should this be the case in any particular area, the local Air Raid Wardens will sound their **HAND RATTLES** to denote the presence of **POISONOUS GAS.**

7. The public in that area should put on their **GAS MASKS** and remain in safety until the **DECONTAMINATION SQUADS** have rendered the area safe.

8. This will be made known by the ringing of **HAND BELLS** by the Air Raid Wardens.

9. **READ THIS OVER CAREFULLY SEVERAL TIMES AND THEN CUT IT OUT AND KEEP FOR REFERENCE FROM TIME TO TIME.**

Darlington now is a wonderful
sight.
We're digging the streets both
by day and by night.
And though Christmas comes
but once every year,
When next Yuletide falls you
will still find us here.

W.D.O

No! They're
not done yet!!

DANGER
ROAD
UP

With love and kisses from the Borough Surveyor
E. Minors, B.Sc., A.M. Inst. C.E.

'Pip', the *Northern Despatch* cartoonist, poked gentle fun at many aspects of Darlington life and its more prominent citizens. This poem, addressed to Ernest Minors, the Borough Surveyor from 1924 to 1947, is as relevant today as when written in December 1927. After his death in 1955 Ernest Minors was commemorated in the name of one of the town's new streets, Minors Crescent.

Two

High Row and Skinnergate

From the appearance of the shops and the almost total absence of pedestrians it would seem that this early 1880s photograph was taken on a Sunday. From the left the shops are: Sidgwick, draper (south of the entrance to Mechanics' Yard); Peter Rhodes, bookseller; Dickson, licensed grocer; Emma Forrest, milliner; Thomas Barker, hosier; and Tom Trattles, jet ornament manufacturer.

In 1901, the year in which the town centre was first lit by electricity, the slope of High Row, Prebend Row and West Row was reconstructed on two levels, making it necessary to erect railings and connecting steps for the safety and convenience of pedestrians. The wooden shelter outside the market hall was built specially for the horse cabmen of the town.

MILWATA RAINCOATS
AT
LUCK & SONS.

These well-known and reliable Raincoats are distinguished not only by their weather resisting properties but also by their perfect fit and smart appearance. Made in every fashionable shade, they are everything that a Raincoat should be, an absolute protection, light in weight, smart and wonderful value.

THE 16/11 RAINCOAT, of good quality Leatherette, fleece lined throughout, double breasted in pretty shades of Tan, Red, Green, Lido

THE 21/- RAINCOAT, an illustrated, colours Nut Brown, New Green, Lido Grey, Red, Navy, Black, Prettyand Fawn.

THE 29/6 RAINCOAT, slightly heavier, made in the present fashionable shades of Light and dark

THE 29/6 RAINCOAT, a special colour number, in Putty and Fawn shades, cut on perfect larger lines.

THE 37/6 RAINCOAT, of reversible Leatherette and Covert Coating, which may be worn to show either side, double breasted in attractive shades of Wine, Almond, Jade, Slate, Brown, Fawn and Navy.

DEXTER RAINCOATS, in a large range of materials, single or Double breasted styles, lined wool checked material, 55/-, 63/- 84/-, absolutely guaranteed in every way.

LUCK & SONS.
HIGH ROW, DARLINGTON

In 1830 Richard Luck and John Watkin commenced trading as Watkin & Luck, drapers, of Horsemarket and High Row. Subsequently the firm was known as Luck & Sons with, at first, two premises on High Row. From the 1920s Luck & Sons concentrated its high-class drapery business in the building next to Barclay's Bank, occupied 1966-2001 by Dressers (Stationers) Ltd and now by a branch of the bookshop chain, Waterstones.

Furnish at BINNS

BIGGEST CHOICE & BEST VALUE

DEFERRED TERMS
to suit Customer's convenience.

BINNS LTD., DARLINGTON.

H. Binns & Co., a Sunderland firm, acquired the Darlington business of Arthur Saunders of 5 High Row in 1922. Over the years Binns took over other premises on High Row and in Blackwellgate to become Darlington's largest department store, although it did not acquire the whole of its present site until 1955.

This map of 1826 shows the area between Bondgate, Blackwellgate, Skinnergate and High Row. The names of some of the property owners can be seen, for example, Mr Clark who gave his name to the still-existing yard and George Allan Esq. of Blackwell Hall and Grange. The numbers refer to some of the town's more important buildings: 6, the Sun Inn; 7, the King's Head Inn; 8, Mr Backhouse's Bank; 9, Mr Skinner's Bank; 10, the Post Office; 14, the Old Fleece Inn; and 15, the Dun Cow Inn.

This small etching was printed at the centre of the five-pound notes issued by Backhouse's Darlington Bank. It shows both the year in which the bank was founded (1774) and a sketch of St Cuthbert's church and the old three-arched bridge over the River Skerne. This particular note was dated in the Quaker style, '22nd of the 10th month 1895', just one year before Backhouse's Bank merged with other private banks to form Barclay & Co. Ltd.

Darlington Bank.

WE, the undersigned Inhabitants of **DARLINGTON**, assure the Country, that we continue to feel the most entire Confidence in the **BANK** of *Jonathan Backhouse & Co.*, and that we take and pay their Notes as usual.

DARLINGTON,

Monday, 8th July, 1816.

Robert Botcherby	William Cudworth	Mary Hird
Edward and Joseph Pease	Thomas Brinby	Thomas Allan
Thomas Clark	John Monkhouse	Jonathan Spark
Thomas Forster	George Towers	John Housfield
Thomas Bowes	Appleby and Sturrow	Henry Smith, senr.
Fra. Mewburn	William Bewick	Ann Robertson
Dennison and Hird	Jacob Brantingham	William Burnet
Thomas Pease	Samuel Forster and Son	George Maxon
William Byerß	James Thompson	Wilson & Johnsons
John Dixon	Thomas Battery	Chr. Thos. & Wm. Dove
William Waters, jun.	Richard Wilson	John Robinson
William Kitching	Anthony Colling	Matthew Nayler
Gordon Skelly, *Hurworth*	Bright Wass	George Nayler
John Theakston, *Ditto*	Green Atkinson	James Topham
Robert Colling, *Ditto*	John Lowis	Frederick Burnett
John Gibson, *Ditto*	John Atkinson	Henry Smith, jun.
Thomas Smorthwaite	William Imson, jun.	Robert Hobson
J. dnd W. Imson and Sons	Jane Scott	James Atkinson
Prescott Pease	John Armitage	William Bell
Pomfret and Middleton	Thomas Tutin	George Boddy
Dobson and Thompson	William Allison	Matthew Nixon
Mary Appleton	Richard Hodgshon	Edward Robson
Harrington Lee	Thomas Taylor	Nathan Robson
Mary Oddie	Robert Harrison	William Robson, jun.
Mary Darnton	Robert Balmer	John Wallas
John Byers	Samuel Greaves	Thomas Pickering
Thomas Craddock	David M'Keown	Matthias Wharrington
George Craddock	Reuben Sanderson	Marshall and Hall
Thomas Wilkinson	Dennison Sanderson	Thomas Horner
Thomas Todhunter	Francis Hall	George Middleton
Lawrence Ridsdale	John Turner	William Crowe
George Heighington	Richard Pickersgill	Francis Harburn
Thomas Fawcett	Allan and Lawton	John Stobbart
John Davison	Joseph Porter	Henry Thompson
Humphrey Thompson		

G. ATKINSON, PRINTER, PREBEND-ROW, DARLINGTON.

Backhouse's Bank, originally in Northgate, took over the High Row premises of Mowbray & Hollingsworth in 1815. Mowbray's 'failed' by not having sufficient bullion with which to redeem its own banknotes when presented. There were frequent panics and subsequent runs on banks in the late eighteenth and early nineteenth centuries. Although Backhouse's Bank survived, there were occasions when it was deemed to be necessary to issue notices proclaiming the confidence of prominent citizens and companies in the integrity of the bank.

This photograph of the middle of High Row, c. 1950, shows, from the right: Lea-Scott, opticians; Anthony Donald, hatters and hosiers; Saxone, shoe retailers; and a branch of Martin's Bank. This bank, founded in Liverpool, was eventually taken over by Barclay's Bank which, for a short time, had two branches on High Row. The building is now occupied by a branch of the Northern Rock Bank.

In 1910 the London City and Midland Bank erected this eye-catching building on the corner of High Row and Bondgate. In 1923 the bank moved into new premises across the road in Prospect Place and the Pearl Assurance Company took over the vacant building. A substantial number of the buildings at the northern end of High Row were demolished in the late 1960s to make way for a mediocre modern development.

The Silver Jubilee of King George V and Queen Mary was celebrated in style in Darlington in 1935. The centre of the town was bedecked with bunting, flags and flowers. The mayor and corporation met to make a loyal address and then processed to St Cuthbert's. As well as school sports, water sports were held in the Gladstone Street public baths and there was an evening firework display in South Park. To mark the occasion male residents of the Municipal Institution (the former workhouse) were given an extra tobacco allowance. Female residents had to be content with a gift of fruit.

This early 1950s photograph of High Row, West Row and Prebend Row, taken from the vantage point of the flat roof of Binns department store, clearly shows the roof line of High Row. A trolley bus waits for passengers on West Row in front of the market hall which will soon have shops built into its west façade.

A gallon of Scotch for 15 shillings! A 1903 advertisement for William Smith Firth, wine, spirit, ale and porter merchant and aerated water manufacturer. At this time, Darlington had 13 wine and spirit merchants, 77 beer retailers and 52 inns and hotels.

No. 67 Skinnergate, c. 1900, with the proprietor Mrs Davison, purveyor of home-made cakes, sweets and biscuits, and her female assistant. Tins of Carr & Co's biscuits, including Marie and People's Mixed, can be seen piled high inside the shop doorway. Until the advent of supermarkets biscuits were sold loose from such tins, shopkeepers obligingly making up 1 lb bags, mixed to their customers' requirements. The site of this shop (opposite Duke Street) is now covered by a modern development. Mrs Davison's husband, a painter and decorator, ran his business from the same address.

Preslands.
Ladies & Gentlemen's Hairdresser
· PERFUMER ·
77 Skinnergate,
DARLINGTON.

Bobbing and Shingling by Experts.

The Finest Hairdressing Saloons in the North.

Fifteen Hairdressers in Attendance.

PRESLANDS 1905.

PORTION OF PRESLANDS 1925.

Right: 'Bobbing and Shingling by Experts'. A 1925 advertisement announcing the opening of Presland's new hairdressing saloons at 77 Skinnergate, on the corner of Buckton's Yard. Originally established in 1905 at 83 Skinnergate, which was acquired to become part of Bainbridge Barker's department store on the corner of Skinnergate and Blackwellgate, Presland's was a well-known name in Darlington until the retirement of Edward D. Presland in 1957. The business was then acquired by another hairdresser, John Hunter.

Below: A closer look at the interior of Presland's gentlemen's hairdressing saloon reveals what would have been considered to be a very upmarket establishment in the 1920s. Prices here would have been far beyond the pocket of the average working man.

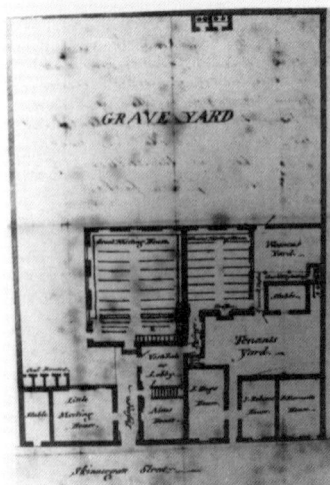

Above: The Religious Society of Friends, popularly known as Quakers, was founded in the 1650s by George Fox. A small group of 'Friends' was established in Darlington by 1666, at first meeting in private houses. Until the passing of the Act of Toleration in 1689 Quakers suffered severely for their beliefs. In this 1838 watercolour by J.M. Sparkes the gables of their two meeting-houses at the southern end of Skinnergate can be seen tucked away behind a row of cottages. It was not until 1840 that the present plain, but imposing, façade was added. On the left can be seen the 'green tree', from which the adjoining inn (and subsequent café) took its name.

Left: A plan showing the layout of the meeting-houses before the addition of the 1840 façade. It was common practice for Quaker meeting-houses and nonconformist chapels to own adjacent property, the rents from which provided income.

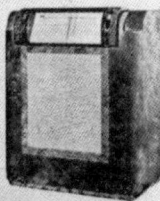

In 1937 Northern Radio and Cycle Supplies offered the latest 'state of the art' valve radios at their shop on the corner of Bell's Place (now occupied by an amusement arcade).

The junction of Grange Road, Coniscliffe Road, Skinnergate and Blackwellgate showing, on the left, the shop and offices of the North of England School Furnishing Company. Opened in 1897 the building was designed by the architect G.G. Hoskins whose hand can still be seen in many of Darlington's public and private buildings. After the company vacated the building in 1954 the ground floor façade was altered to accommodate a branch of Lloyds Bank.

Three

Blackwellgate, Coniscliffe Road and Grange Road

It is difficult to believe that Blackwellgate formed part of the Great North Road (A1) from this 1900 photograph. It is also surprising to see that the well-known landmark, the clock of the Northern Goldsmiths, once adorned the shop of the jewellers, Richardson & Co. on the opposite side of the street. On the left can be seen Mrs Wheeler's, ladies' outfitter and Black's, butchers, next to the unassuming façade of the Three Blue Bells Hotel. On the right are the lion-surmounted premises of Priestman & Son, monumental masons.

Ten years later a very different scene meets the eye. Blackwellgate (but not Houndgate) has acquired electric light, the Three Blue Bells is adorned with a stepped gable, and the clock has crossed the road. The general hustle and bustle and the presence of a horse omnibus and carriers' carts and wagons suggests that it is market day.

Above: A sunny Blackwellgate in the 1950s, with a run of shop sun-blinds, a possible hazard to the drivers of large lorries on the A1. The Fleece Hotel, closed in 1968, was demolished to make way for the uninspiring frontage of Boyes' departmental store. The premises of B. Jackson, house furnishers and Aitkens, fish and game dealer survive, the former converted into the (so far) hard-to-let Houndgate Mews and the latter, with a new façade, occupied by Guru. The rest of the buildings on the right have been demolished to make way for modern development.

Right: Sydney H. Wood stands in the doorway of his fine art gallery and photographic studio in Blackwellgate, c. 1915. Reputed to be the finest photographer in Darlington, his services were much in demand to capture the town's citizens and events for posterity. It is a great pity that many of his negatives were lost when the firm moved in the 1950s after the premises were acquired by Binns.

Hours 9 to 6. Saturdays 9 to 1.   Telephone 2468.

SYDNEY H. WOOD, Photographic Studio.
Fine Art Gallery, Darlington.

ARTISTIC PORTRAITURE.   CHILD PORTRAITE.

Coloured Miniatures.—Orders executed on Ivory, Ivorine, or Paper. Artists of acknowledged skill and taste retained. Old Miniatures copied or restored. Special attention given to Copying. Old and Faded Photographs and Daguerreotypes can be copied or enlarged and finished in any process.

CONISCLIFFE ROAD DARLINGTON

146

According to its caption this postcard shows the altar of the church of St Augustus, Darlington. The Catholic church of St Augustine, tucked away behind Coniscliffe Road, was built on a corner of the Green Tree Field and opened for worship in 1827. The retablum (or reredos), installed in 1899, is made of Austrian oak and is said to be one of the finest in the north-east.

Opposite above: Coniscliffe Road in the 1920s, cobbled and without a motor vehicle in sight. Most of the houses on the left were demolished in the 1930s to make way for a garage on the corner of West Street (recently replaced by a block of 'luxury apartments'). Fortunately the trees in the background in the grounds of Larchfield have survived both the house's transition into a school and its eventual demolition to make way for a modern social club.

Opposite below: This house, which can also be seen in the right foreground of the previous photograph, was demolished as recently as 1985 to make way for Hogarth Court, one of several housing developments in the town by the Darlington Housing Association (formerly Re-Roof). The attractive curved brick wall to the left has been retained and incorporated into the design. Behind it can be seen the small building which served as a Catholic chapel before the building of St Augustine's church.

The children of St Augustine's, c. 1908, marshalled outside the County Court building in Coniscliffe Road before taking part in a procession of witness around the parish. In the centre of the photograph is Monsignor James Rooney, the parish priest from 1876 until his death in September 1931. He is buried in West Cemetery.

Opposite above: In June 1928 the Sir E.D. Walker Homes in Coniscliffe Road were opened by Lady Aberdeen, accompanied by her husband, the Marquess of Aberdeen and Temair. Also present at the ceremony were the Bishop of Durham, Dr Hensley Henson; the Conservative Parliamentary candidate, Viscount Castlereagh; Sir Hugh Bell; Arthur Shepherd, MP for Darlington; the mayor, Councillor S Hardwick; and William Heslop, the senior trustee of the homes.

Below: Sir Edward Daniel Walker, who died on 21 May 1919, came to Darlington as a boy to work for the Stockton and Darlington Railway. Later, he founded the wholesale newsagents' business of E.D. Walker & Wilson and, for a time, was the chief proprietor of The Northern Echo. He was three times Mayor of Darlington and was knighted in 1908. In his will he bequeathed £60,000 to build almshouses on land near the junction of Coniscliffe Road and Carmel Road South, acquired from John William Pease. The final development differed somewhat from this architect's drawing.

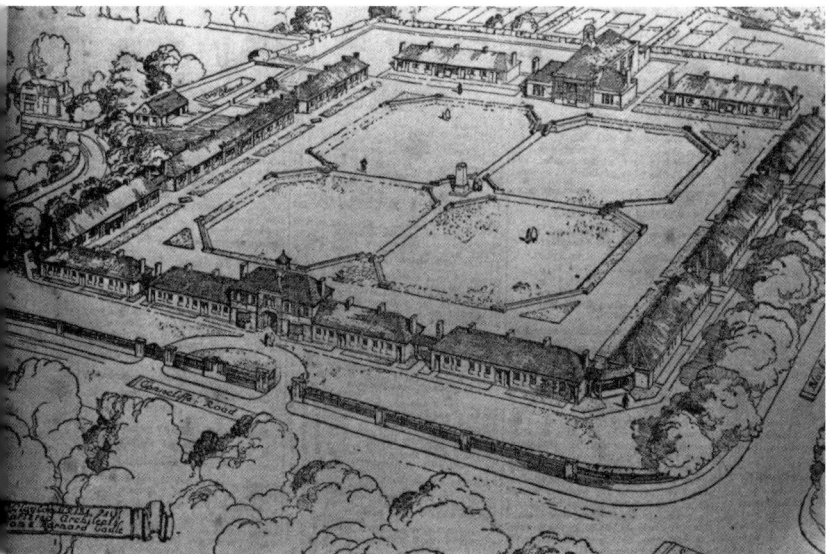

Woodside, one of Darlington's many minor 'stately homes', was situated in extensive grounds between Coniscliffe Road and Blackwell Lane. Originally built as a modest house in the 1830s, it was greatly enlarged in the late 1840s after its purchase by John Harris. Harris, a Quaker, was one of the instigators of the Freeholders' Estate in the Eastbourne area of the town and gave his name to one of its streets. The name of Woodside lives on in Woodside Drive, built on the site of the house which was demolished in 1938 for housing development.

John, the eldest son of Edward Pease, 'Father of Railways', had two similar houses built near to Salutation Corner on Coniscliffe Road: Elm Ridge as a home for himself, his wife and unmarried daughter, and Woodburn (shown here) as a home for his elder daughter, Sophia, and her husband, Theodore Fry. Unfortunately, John Pease died in 1868 before Elm Ridge was completed. Woodburn was demolished in 1935.

Opposite below: This photograph of Kilbucho, at the corner of Cleveland Avenue and Langholm Crescent, was probably taken by an itinerant photographer in the hope that the occupants would be interested in buying postcards which depicted their new home.

Sophia Pease was born in June 1837 at East Mount, the home of her parents, John and Sophia Pease. For most of her adult life she was involved in philanthropic and educational work. In August 1862 she married Theodore Fry of Bristol and set up home in a house called Woodburn. In 1866, when the Frys moved to the house built for them at Salutation Corner, the name of their old home was transferred to the new. Theodore Fry, the town's MP from 1880 to 1895, was created a baronet in 1894. Lady Fry died in Biarritz in 1897 and is buried in the Friends' Cemetery behind Skinnergate Meeting-house.

With kind regards.

Sir Theodore Fry,

Woodburn,
Darlington.

The simple black-edged mourning card used by Sir Theodore Fry. After the death of his wife he eventually left Darlington and remarried in 1902. He died at Caterham in February 1912, aged 75.

In 1870 Joseph Pease presented the town with 'Southend' (the name of his villa, now the Grange Hotel), a horse-drawn steam pump fire-engine. It was housed in the cellars under the market hall. Here the fire-engine is being tested at the town's waterworks in Coniscliffe Road, opposite Jubilee Cottages. This section of the waterworks is now maintained by the Tees Cottage Pumping Station Preservation Society which holds regular open days.

The Newly-Elected Mayor of Darlington.
(T. M. BARRON, ESQ.)

Thomas Metcalfe Barron (1852–1916) was born in Darlington. In 1875, he became a solicitor (T.M. Barron & Smith, Church Row) and was elected as a Conservative town councillor in 1884, serving as chairman of both the Public Library and Gas Committees. On becoming mayor in 1890 he organized a huge 'At Home' in South Park, to which the entire population of Darlington was invited. In 1909 he was given the freedom of the town.

Postcards depicting life at Polam Hall School are many and varied. No doubt they were popular with boarders who were required to write regularly to their parents—so much quicker to write than a letter and the postage was cheaper. Here, five pupils have posed in front of the ivy-covered games shed. The school was first established in 1848 at Selby House, 11 Houndgate, before moving to Polam Hall in 1854.

Woodside Terrace, Grange Road was the home of the Training College for Elementary School Mistresses for almost four years, from February 1872 to December 1875 when the college moved to new, purpose-built premises in Vane Terrace (now the Arts Centre). Between 1900 and 1905, as the houses fell vacant, Polam Hall School became the tenant of almost the entire terrace, using one house as accommodation for its headmistress and the rest as overflow accommodation for the school (Polam House).

Above: George Allan, general merchant of Darlington, was born in Yarm in 1663. He is said to have built or 're-edified' Blackwell Grange in 1710 and to have added the south wing in 1717 on the occasion of his son George's marriage to an heiress, Thomasine Prescott. On the death of George Thomas Allan, 'the last scion of the Allan family', in November 1885 at the age of 87, the house and estate was inherited by his cousin, Henry Havelock, who adopted the name of Allan. The house remained in the hands of the Havelock-Allans until it was sold and converted into a hotel.

Left: Henry Marshman Havelock was born in India in 1830, the son of an army officer. Both father and son fought in the wars of the Indian Mutiny, Henry receiving the Victoria Cross for his part in the storming of the Charbagh Bridge in September 1857. A baronetcy was conferred on him in 1858. On succeeding to the estates of his cousin, George Thomas Allan in 1885, he assumed the name Allan by Royal Licence. In December 1897 he was killed in the Khyber Pass.

'Pip', the *Northern Despatch* cartoonist, often used Darlington's more eminent citizens as subjects. This cartoon of 1929 portrays Sir Henry Spencer Moreton Havelock-Allan (1872–1953) who had succeeded to the baronetcy in 1897. After an army career Sir Henry played his part in local affairs, serving as a town councillor, a District Commissioner for Scouts and as MP for Bishop Auckland for eight years. A keen horseman, Sir Henry rode with the Zetland, South Durham and Hurworth hunts.

A sketch of the Punch Bowl Inn at the corner of Blackwell and Carmel Road South, drawn by Alfred B. Dresser, a well-known Darlington artist. The inn (now a private house) later became the farmhouse for Blackwell Grange Farm.

Blackwell Bridge, designed by John Green of Newcastle, was opened in 1832 as a toll-bridge. It was built to shorten the journey from Darlington to Richmond, traffic previously having to use the bridge at Croft. Unfortunately the toll trustees were unable to recoup their investment after the opening of the Richmond branch of the Great North of England Railway in September 1846 siphoned off much of the traffic. The bridge was widened in 1961 to cope with the demands of traffic on the Great North Road.

Four

Bondgate, Woodland Road and Cockerton

Bondgate in the early 1950s, the Prospect Place branch of the Midland Bank exhorting the town's citizens to invest in National Saving Certificates. Beyond the bank are the premises of Sidney E. Taylor, photographer; Charles, costumiers; K. Stanton, boot and shoe dealers; and Amos Hinton & Sons, grocers. The statue of Joseph Pease, on its original site in the middle of the road, gazes down High Row.

This photograph of an almost traffic-free Bondgate in the 1920s shows the extreme width of its eastern section. The splendid motor-cycle combination is parked outside the shop of G. Prudhoe, newsagent and tobacconist. On the other side of Kearton's Yard are the premises of T. Pemberton, fruiterer and florist. F.W. Bucktin, chemist occupied the shop on the western corner of Skinnergate.

The north side of Bondgate, showing a huge, multi-armed 'telegraph' pole. With the advent of underground cabling these poles have become obsolete, but the town's last remaining one in Buckton's Yard was not removed until as late as 1991. The large, three-storey building in the centre of the row, under which was the entrance to Potter's Yard, housed J. Shutt, printer. It is now occupied by the estate agents, Sanderson, Townend and Gilbert. The rest of the row to its left was demolished in the 1960s.

Trams were officially superseded by trolley buses in April 1926. The advent of the 'trackless tram' made tram lines in the centre of the road redundant and in Bondgate the available space was used as parking for the increasing number of motor vehicles. The town's trolley bus routes were lined with rows of poles to support the wires which carried electric current to the vehicles, cluttering both pavement and skyline.

On 10 June 1862 the Darlington Total Abstinence Society unveiled a drinking fountain
in the centre of Bondgate, opposite the entrance to Skinnergate, to commemorate its first
president, John Fothergill MRCS, who had died in January 1858. Dr Fothergill had lived on
the north side of Bondgate. The fountain was moved to South Park in 1875.

Abbott's Apothecaries' Hall stood on the south side of Bondgate near its junction with High Row. Founded in the 1860s, it was taken over by R. Nicholson who, like all chemists of the day, prepared and sold his 'own name' pills and potions.

The Society of Friends opposed the sale of alcohol and actively supported temperance organizations. Some local Quakers formed the Coffee Cart Company of Darlington to provide non-alcoholic refreshment at a modest price throughout the town. In this specially posed photograph of the 1870s the coffee cart stands on the south side of Bondgate, near to the entrance to Salt Yard.

In the late nineteenth century, dancing bears provided popular street entertainment, the poor creatures being trained to 'dance' when their keeper was given money by the spectators. This particular performance took place in front of the offices of the Ecclesiastical Commissioners in Bondgate. The house on the right still stands on the corner of Bondgate and Archer Street, but the others were demolished to make way for the 1932 Majestic (later Odeon) Cinema, now Riley's Snooker Hall.

Rotary Club, Darlington

BAZAAR

In aid of the Y.M.C.A.
In Bondgate Wesleyan
Memorial Hall (kindly lent by the Trustees)
Wednesday, Thursday
April 18 & 19, 1928

The Darlington branch of the Young Men's Christian Association which had been founded in 1868 was housed in West Lodge, Woodland Road in 1928. The Bondgate Wesleyan Methodist Hall was built as a memorial to the members of the church who had been killed in the First World War.

In spite of threat of demolition in both 1968 and 1975, the Britannia Inn still stands in the remnant of Archer Street which, before the construction of St Augustine's Way, connected Bondgate and Gladstone Street.

Joseph Malaby Dent, the tenth child of George Dent, was born in August 1849 in the house in Archer Street which was later to become the Britannia Inn. At the age of 13 he was apprenticed to a printer, and later to a bookbinder. In 1867 he was sent to London to complete his apprenticeship with 2s 6d in his pocket. After establishing his own publishing business, he founded the Everyman Library in 1906. A member of the council of the British & Foreign School Society, he purchased Fairfield in Woodland Road in 1918, for use as a practising nursery school by the students of the Training College in Vane Terrace.

IN MEMORY OF
GEORGE DENT
BORN 27 M^{ar} 1810
DIED 27 M^{ay} 1878

ALSO OF JOSEPH
MALABY DENT
BORN 30 A^{ug} 1849
DIED 9 M^{ay} 1926

The plaque to the memory of George and Joseph Malaby Dent which is in the porch of Fairfield, now the George Dent Nursery School.

Lynton House Preparatory School, c. 1936. Established at 10 Stanhope Road in 1925 by Hilda L. Furniss, the school opened with just four pupils. By the time Miss Furniss retired in 1966, the school had sixty pupils and four members of staff.

A group of students at the North of England College for the Training of Mistresses in Elementary Schools in Vane Terrace. Their teacher (centre front) was Miss Jane Grenfell who taught at the college from 1900 to 1934.

The Free Grammar School of Queen Elizabeth and the North of England College, side by side in Vane Terrace. Since 1874 the town council had been represented on the grammar school's board of governors. The affairs of the training college were handled by a committee of twenty-four, whose first chairman was Theodore Fry.

The Teacher Training College, opened in 1875, was designed by James Pigott Pritchett, a member of a family of architects, who had established his practice in Darlington. After the closure of the college in 1978 the decision was taken to establish the town's Arts Centre there, said to be largest in the country. The glass corridor is now used as an exhibition area.

West Lodge now suffers the ignominy of being hidden behind the Job Centre in Woodland Road. Originally the home of members of the Backhouse family, it became the home of David Dale after his marriage in 1853 to a widow, Annie Whitwell, née Annie Backhouse Robson. David Dale, who was created a baronet in 1895, was managing director of the Consett Iron Company, a partner in Pease & Partners, and a director of the North Eastern Railway.

Trinity chapel was built as a chapel-of-ease in the parish of St Cuthbert, partly as a result of requests from the inhabitants of Cockerton for a church of their own. Built to the designs of Anthony Salvin, an architect of national repute, the foundation stone was laid in October 1836. The separate parish of Holy Trinity was created in April 1843.

Woodland(s) Road, once a rural tram route to Cockerton, lost its final 's' c. 1910. The stair turret of the tower of Holy Trinity church can just be seen behind a veritable thicket of trees. The Cockerton tram is just passing Balmoral Terrace.

The children's ward (built 1897), Greenbank Hospital, c. 1930. The hospital, supported by voluntary contributions, bed-endowments and constant fund-raising efforts, opened in 1885. It soon proved to be too small for the town's needs and, after the First World War, the decision was taken to build a new hospital as a war memorial. Used as the town's maternity hospital until the opening of the maternity unit of the Memorial Hospital in September 1989, Greenbank was demolished in 1994 to make way for sheltered housing.

The foundation stone of the War Memorial Hospital was laid in June 1926 by Lord Daryngton (Herbert Pike Pease). This photograph shows the crowds who gathered on 5 May 1933 to watch Prince George (later the Duke of Kent) lay a commemorative stone. Both the foundation and commemorative stones can still be seen, flanking the entrance door of the administation block.

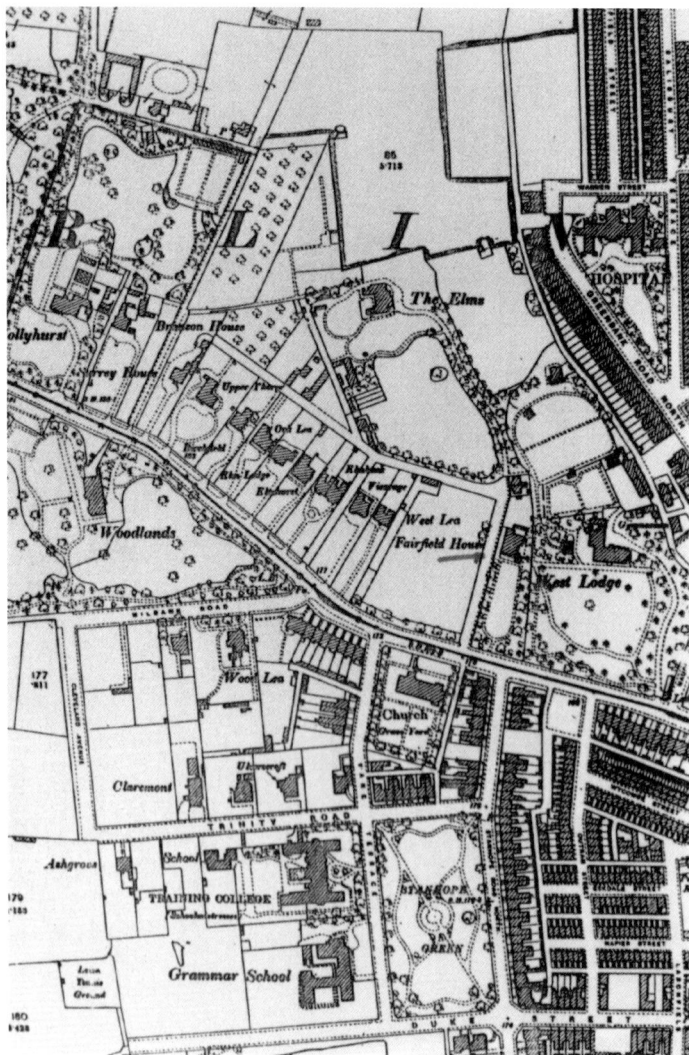

A map of 1898, showing Greenbank Hospital, West Lodge, standing in its own grounds, and the row of substantial villas which once graced the north side of Woodland Road. The Elms and its extensive estate was purchased to provide the site for the War Memorial Hospital. The house was demolished in 1930 but its name lives on in the small street opposite Holy Trinity church.

DARLINGTON GENERAL HOSPITAL.

GARDEN FETE

TO BE

HELD AT THE ELMS

(Site for the New Hospital, entrance from Woodland Road),

On Wednesday, Sept. 7th, 1927,

AT 2-30 P.M.

ADMISSION SIXPENCE.

Above: Until the introduction of the National Health Service in July 1948, the hospitals in Darlington were supported by the generosity of the townspeople. Special events, organized by voluntary societies and organizations, flag days, weekly deductions from wages and the biannual Railwaymen's Carnival all contributed towards the cost of providing hospital facilities for the town and surrounding area.

Right: Prince George, accompanied by Councillor William Heslop, in the grounds of the Sir E.D. Walker Homes in Coniscliffe Road, 5 May 1933. Councillor Heslop, the homes' senior trustee, had been the Mayor of Darlington in 1931/2 and is one of the few people to have been granted the honour of the freedom of the town.

The Woodlands, the house after which the road to Cockerton was named, was built in 1815 by Robert Botcherby. By 1854 it had become the home of the newly married Joseph Whitwell Pease, who six years later extended the house to almost double its original size. This photograph shows part of the estate, much of which was sold for housing development in 1908. The Woodlands (for several years the HQ of the Wilshier Group) is now occupied by St Teresa's Hospice which has recently launched a major appeal to fund the accomodation and expansion of its counselling and therapy services.

Joseph Whitwell Pease (1828–1903), the eldest son of Joseph Pease, served as MP for South Durham from 1865 to 1885 and as MP for Barnard Castle from 1885 until his death. In 1882 he became a baronet, the first Quaker to accept such an honour. He eventually moved to Hutton Hall near Guisborough, which had been built for him by Alfred Waterhouse, the architect of Barclay's Bank and the market hall. He died in Falmouth in June 1903 and is buried in the Friends' Cemetery, Skinnergate.

Above: The Drovers Garage stands on the site of the Drovers' Inn, which once may have provided shelter and refreshment for the men and women whose job it was to drive cattle and sheep to market. The inn's licence was transferred to the nearby Travellers' Rest in 1926 and the buildings, converted for use as a garage in 1936, survived until 1965 when they were replaced by a more modern structure (recently demolished for further development).

Left: St Mary's church was built in 1901 to fulfil the long-expressed wish of the Anglican residents of Cockerton to have a church of their own. When Edward Thomas Pease, wine merchant, died in 1897, he bequeathed £4,000 to the church and parish of Holy Trinity, part of which was used to purchase the site of the Cockerton church.

Mary Jane Allen was the star equestrian performer in her husband's travelling Excelsior Circus, which was accustomed to pitch its tents on the field to the rear of the Green Tree Inn in Skinnergate. During the circus's visit to the town in 1874 Mary Jane Allen died, and she was buried in West Cemetery, her husband erecting this magnificent memorial to her memory. Although now badly weathered, the monument can still be seen in the plot to the south of the cemetery's chapels.

The site of Hazel Avenue, between Brinkburn Road and Willow Road, formed part of the Brinkburn estate of Henry Fell Pease. This postcard, date stamped July 1914, shows the newly erected houses and an unsurfaced road.

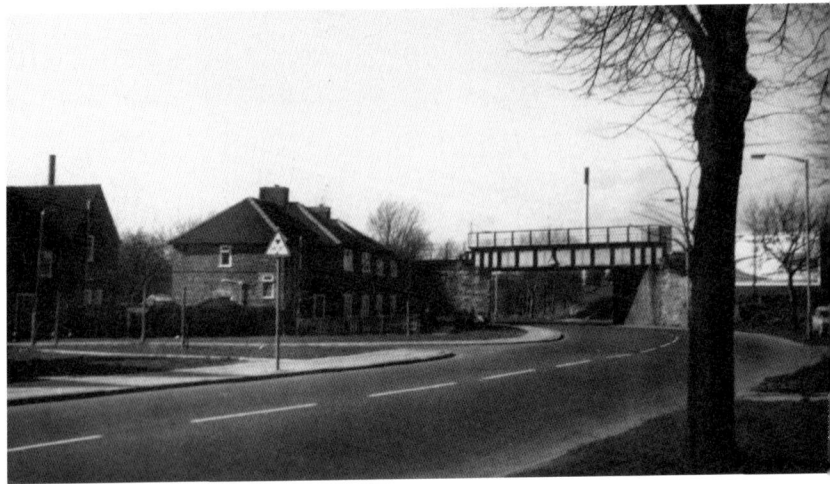

The railway bridge over West Auckland Road was built to carry the Darlington and Barnard Castle Railway which opened in July 1856. The line also served the Chemical and Insulating Company's works which opened in 1927. The line closed in 1966 but the bridge, despite being a constant hazard to high vehicles, was not demolished until 1983.

Five

Prospect Place and Northgate

The King's Head has been in existence since before 1661, when its purchase by Sir John Lowther is recorded. From 1770 it was a coaching stop for the Newcastle Post Coach which ran between London and Newcastle. The entrance to the inn's stable yard can be seen behind the statue of Joseph Pease. The last coach ran in 1852. The inn was demolished and replaced by the present hotel which opened in June 1893.

This ornate gas lamp had originally stood in the market-place, being erected to commemorate the coronation of William IV in 1830. Moved to Prospect Place in 1862, it was again displaced in 1875 to make way for the statue of Joseph Pease. Behind the lamp can be seen the Joint Stock Bank, founded in 1831 to compete with privately owned banks, and (on the right) the Sun Inn.

Both the King's Head Hotel and the Sun Inn provided hearses and mourning coaches for hire. Mr Wrightson's advertisement specifically mentions the 'new' cemetery, but as the first burial had taken place in June 1858 West Cemetery was not exactly new when this edition of the Darlington Telegraph was published. In advertising the proximity of his hostelry to both the county court in Coniscliffe Road and the police station in Grange Road, Joseph Marshall of the Black Bull Inn, on the corner of Blackwellgate and Grange Road, was obviously hoping to attract the custom of the legal fraternity, and its clients.

The Sun Inn was demolished in 1867 to make way for an imposing extension to the Joint Stock Bank and to enable the narrow entrance to Northgate to be widened.

In 1923 the Prospect Place bank buildings, by then owned by the Midland Bank (now HSBC), were demolished and the present building constructed to the designs of Brierley and Rutherford of York. The opportunity was again taken to improve the access to Northgate, the entrance being widened by two feet.

The bank under construction in 1923.
Until it reopened, Midland Bank customers
were able to use the facilities of the branch
on the corner of High Row and Bondgate
(see p. 25).

An 1903 advertisement for A.W. Ison,
chemist, which occupied one of the six
shops in the King's Head Buildings in
Prebend Row.

73

A branch of Marks and Spencer's Penny Bazaar, whose advertising slogan was 'You don't need to ask the price. It's a penny,' opened at 8 Prospect Place in December 1911 with a staff of eight (shown here). The manageress, Miss Violet Rutter is fourth from the left.

Opposite above: Northgate in 1910. On the right can be seen the elegant railings of the offices of Pease & Partners, complemented by the equally elegant balcony of the Three Tuns Inn opposite. Beyond is the post office (now a branch of Dorothy Perkins) and the row of three shops which alone have survived the ruthless onslaught of the modern developer in this section of Northgate.

Below: Northgate, c. 1860. The building on the left served as the post office until its demolition to make way for the entrance to Crown Street, when business was transferred to the new, custom-built post office shown in the previous photograph. To its right are the offices of the Great North of England Railway which connected Darlington to York and from there, via other railways, to London.

J. Hawitt, who died in December 1955, came from Macclesfield to be Head Postmaster of Darlington from 1936 to 1943. During the Second World War he was in charge of the GPO detachment of the Home Guard.

Some of the Gas Fitters and Fittings Inspectors.

Darlington Corporation was justly proud of its municipal undertakings and staff. This 1937 photograph shows some of the town's gas fitters and inspectors with their supervisor, J. S. Tiplady, at the John Street depot.

Beauty's Contour

Denotes all that supreme excellence in Corset Shape and Fit so much sought after. The New Models represent all that is possible in the art of Modern Corset manufacture. Further, the supports are guaranteed to be absolutely rustless.

Prices from 2/11½ to 8/11 per pair.

MILLINER, FANCY DRAPER, AND CORSET SPECIALIST.

Type 218, 8/11.

Frank Britton, 18, Northgate, Darlington.
(CORNER OF UNION STREET)

Above: Rustproof corsets for only 2s 11½d! The more discerning ladies of the town must have made a beeline for 18 Northgate.

Right: If it was made of rubber the Archer Rubber Company of 20 Northgate, renowned for the 'Keepudry' raincoat, sold it.

INDIARUBBER

Hose Pipes.
Washers.
Insertion Sheet.
Gas Tubing.
Inner Tubes.
Pram Tyres.
Hot Water Bags.
Air Cushions.
Water Pillows.
Enema Syringes.
Mats for Traps,
&c.

WATERPROOF

Garments.
Carriage Rugs.
Bed Sheetings.
Loin Covers.
Aprons.
Fishing Waders.
Wellingtons.
Snow Shoes.
Goloshes.
Mining Boots.
Leggings,
&c.

THIS IS THE DEPOT FOR THE NOTED

'KEEPUDRY' MACINTOSHES
(Guaranteed for all Climates.)

The ARCHER   RUBBER Co.,
20, Northgate,   DARLINGTON.

77

Northgate in 1890. Horse tram No. 11 makes its leisurely way past Ivy House which served as the headquarters of the Darlington Liberal Unionist Association. J. Dodds, printer, on the corner of Kendrew Street and Northgate, printed and published many of the pictorial postcards of Darlington.

Opposite: The A.B. Chocolate Company had two branches in Darlington, a subsidiary one in Blackwellgate (now part of a branch of Thomas Cook) and the main one in Northgate (now Best Kebab 1). On the bay window of this building can still be seen the two tile plaques commemorating Edward Pease, its former owner, and the part he played in the nation's transport history. Passers-by could be forgiven for thinking that the 'Father of Railways' had lived in a small, rather ugly, tile-fronted house. In fact his house (now subdivided and partly hidden by later façades and shop fronts) occupied the whole block.

The house where Edward
Pease resided in 1820.

The first Public Railway
was inaugurated here.

The Premises are now occupied by

The A.B. Chocolate Co.,

Who only sell the Highest Quality
CHOCOLATES AND SWEETMEATS.

Branch Shop:
30 BLACKWELLGATE.

The little White Shop with the
250 year old window.

Edward Pease, born in Darlington in May 1767, was educated in Leeds before joining the family woollen business. In 1796 he married Rachel Whitwell of Kendal. The marriage was to produce five sons and three daughters. After he retired in 1817 Edward directed his energies to promoting what was to become the Stockton and Darlington Railway, earning him the title of 'Father of Railways'. Both Rachel (d. October 1833) and Edward (d. July 1858) are buried in the Friends' Cemetery in Skinnergate.

George Hudson, born in 1880, was a York draper who became a wealthy man after inheriting a large quantity of railway shares. In 1837 he was appointed as lord mayor of York. Together with Joseph Pease he was responsible for the building of the railway between Darlington and York and was invited to lay the foundation stone of the church of St John the Evangelist at Bank Top, Darlington. In 1849 Hudson, the 'Railway King', was forced to resign all his offices when it was discovered that he had been misappropriating the money of railway shareholders.

FRANCIS MEWBURN. 1785—1867.
First Railway Solicitor and
last Bailiff of Darlington.

Among the small group of men who pioneered the formation of the Stockton and Darlington Railway Company, Francis Mewburn, solicitor, deserves especial credit. He furthered the progress of railways for over forty years, from 1817 to 1860. In 1846 he was appointed by the Bishop of Durham to serve as the chief bailiff of Darlington and managed the town's affairs until 1850, when a Local Government Board was formed. He lived at Larchfield in Coniscliffe Road until his death in 1867.

THOS. MCNAY,
First Secretary, S. & D. R.

JOHN DIXON. 1796—1865.
Surveyor, S. & D.R.

Above left: Thomas McNay, born in Wallsend in 1810, was employed as a boy by the firm of Hawthorns, engine manufacturers, before coming to Darlington to work for the Stockton and Darlington Railway Company (S&DR). A man of ability, he soon rose to the position of secretary to the S&DR and other railways. A town councillor and president of the Railway Institute in Northgate, he died in August 1869 allegedly from overwork, and is buried in West Cemetery.

Above right: John Dixon, another local railway pioneer, was born in Cockfield. He assisted George Stephenson in the surveying and building of both the S&DR and the Liverpool and Manchester railway. He became the engineer-in-chief of the S&DR in the 1840s, living at Belle Vue, Coniscliffe Road. He died in October 1865 and is buried in West Cemetery.

Opposite above: A parade of men, passing the Queen's Nurses' Home in Northgate, on their way to the town centre. Their well-drilled appearance gives the impression that this might have been a march of 'old comrades' after the First World War.

Opposite below: A School of Art had existed in Darlington since at least 1857. For many years the classes were held in the Mechanics' Institute in Skinnergate, with separate classes, both daytime and evening, for 'ladies' and 'gentlemen' but evening classes only for 'artizans'. When the new Technical College was opened in Northgate it incorporated the School of Art. One of the statues on the top of the building is said to represent Art.

SCHOOL OF ART,
DARLINGTON.

DARLINGTON

Darlington's Technical College, designed by G.G. Hoskins, was opened in October 1897 by the Duke of Devonshire. The ceremonial key used can still be seen at the duke's ancestral home, Chatsworth. In 1916 the YMCA (signposted in this photograph) was accommodated in a hut in North Lodge Park. There was also a canteen for soldiers in Union Street.

Opposite above: Northgate, looking south, in the late 1880s. The gateway on the right of this photograph marks the point where Gladstone Street now joins Northgate. When the Technical College was built the line of Gladstone Street was extended eastwards.

Opposite below: The entrance to the Technical College, flanked by two very elegant gas lamps. The horse and cart wait next to the Bulmer Stone, Darlington's oldest 'monument'. A huge piece of Shap granite, it is believed to have rested here since it was brought across the Pennines and then deposited by a glacier. In 1923 it was deemed to be a hazard to traffic and 'imprisoned' behind the college railings, where it lay for many years, largely ignored. In 1992 a fact sheet relating its history was fixed to the college wall.

SWISS CHALET, BRINKBURN DENE, DARLINGTON.

'Swiss chalets' were popular features in many public parks. This example stood in Brinkburn Dene, close to Willow Road and Hamsterley, Acacia and Coniston Streets. This part of the Brinkburn estate, which had been purchased from Walter Fell Pease in 1912, was known as Cockerbeck Valley. At first used as allotments it was opened as a recreation ground in September 1925.

Opposite: A 1915 advertisement for Tom Horsfall, funeral director, who lived over the shop in High Northgate. Strictly speaking his correct address would have been 8 Livingstone Buildings, High Northgate, as all the terraces on the west side of the Great North Road had individual names.

TOM HORSFALL,

Certified Embalmer

and Funeral Director.

The only Firm in the District that are FUNERAL
FURNISHERS exclusively.

All Coffins, Shrouds, &c., are made at our own works
Wreaths, Crosses, &c., a Speciality.

RESIDENCE AND SHOW ROOMS:

8, High Northgate, DARLINGTON.

(Next to the Assembly Hall),

WORKS : WOOLER STREET.

☞ DAY AND NIGHT ATTENDANCE,

The Trade also supplied with Coffins, Shrouds, and
every requisite.

Telegrams: "HORSFALL, DARLINGTON.

A busy High Northgate, c. 1910. At this point a crossover for trams terminating at the Theatre Royal and then returning to the town centre was built, but never used. Its filled-in outline can just be seen in the foreground. On the right can be seen the shops of E. Scunthorpe, confectioner; E. Gale, newsagent & tobacconist; J. Waters, pharmacist; and Walter Willson, multiple grocer.

Above: The North Road Locomotive Works of the North Eastern Railway opened on 1 January 1863 and occupied approximately 20 acres by the turn of the century. Fronting North Road were the offices and stores. The works closed on 2 April 1966, just a few years after this photograph was taken.

Right: Immediately before the First World War the North Eastern Railway employed over 2,250 men in the works. During the war part of the workshops, under the impressive title of the Darlington National Projectile Factory, was used for the manufacture of munitions. Over 1,000 women were employed there.

Durham Road was the name given to the portion of North Road between Cumberland Street and the borough boundary at Harrowgate Hill. This postcard of around 1926 shows Mrs C.A. Hutchinson's confectioners shop and, on the opposite corner of Ruby Street, the Primitive Methodist church. The eastern side of Durham Road was still largely undeveloped.

Six

The Market, Tubwell Row and Bank Top

The town clock looks down on an almost deserted Tubwell Row. On the right can be seen the premises of D. McNaughton, dyer and Salter & Salter Ltd, bootmakers, and the entrance to Raby Yard and the Raby Hotel. Higher up Tubwell Row were two further yards, Crabtree's and Harrison's. The water pump which can be seen opposite East Row does not mark the site of the well from which the street got its name. The site of the Tub Well was rediscovered opposite Church Row during the final stages of the building of the Cornmill Centre.

A view of Horsemarket in the early 1950s from Binns department store, the skyline punctured by the three electricity cooling towers, St Cuthbert's spire, St John's tower and the bulk of the Central Hall. On the right are the shops of J. Lear, ironmonger, and W.H. Smith.

A parade to boost fund raising for the war effort during the Second World War, with the Civil Defence Corps marching up Horsemarket.

Copyright.

THE OLD TOWN HALL, DARLINGTON,

The foundation stone of which was laid by George Allan, Esq., of Blackwell Grange, on the 13th April, 1808, and was pulled down to make room for the Covered Market, in February, 1863.

Published by W. J. Oliver, 5 Parkgate, Darlington.

The Old Town Hall stood at the top of Tubwell Row, roughly on the site of the town clock tower.

This photograph, taken from High Row in 1864, shows the nearly completed market hall clock tower, still awaiting the installation of its clock, the gift of Joseph Pease. The market hall opened for business at 7 a.m. on 2 May 1864, the first customer being Mr Wrightson of the Sun Inn, Prospect Place who bought a leg of mutton.

In 1856 the Board of Health, Darlington's first elected local government, bought the market rights (which had formerly belonged to the Bishop of Durham) from the Ecclesiastical Commissioners. Despite opposition from many of the ratepayers the decision was taken to build a new town hall with an adjoining market hall, to the designs of Alfred Waterhouse, a nationally known architect who was related to the Darlington Pease family.

Waterhouse's town hall of 1864 soon proved to be too small to accommodate the town's new council, brought into being by the charter of 1867, and supporting staff. The number of councillors increased in 1915 when Darlington became a County Borough and again in 1930. This photograph shows the cramped conditions of the council chamber. It was to be 1970 before conditions improved on the opening of the present town hall.

The market square, February 1978. Improvements in the standards of food handling and hygiene eventually made the upgrading of the market hall's facilities essential. The stallholders were dispossessed and the interior gutted. In the mean time the stallholders had to face the rigour of two winters in the temporary accommodation erected in the market square.

Darlington's Monday and Saturday market days attract traders and shoppers alike from a wide surrounding area. This photograph shows the stalls under the East Row market canopy and on Bakehouse Hill in the late 1950s.

During the course of the market hall's refurbishment the opportunity was taken to carry out repair work to the clock tower, the resulting scaffolding and staging giving it a very 'space age' appearance.

Market day, Bakehouse Hill, c. 1890. From right to left: the Market Hotel, Mason's Dining Rooms, the Bull's Head Hotel, and Pease's Wine Shop.

Darlington—
Between you and me
this is a jolly place.

The market-place, c. 1910. An extension has been added to the Market Hotel and the shop of Thomas Pease and Son has been rebuilt. The corrugated iron building on the left housed the agricultural supplies depot of Ord & Maddison Ltd.

The Deanery, on the right, was demolished in 1876. Before the Reformation the clergy of the church of St Cuthbert had consisted of a dean and four prebends. On the left can be seen the houses adjoining the Hat and Feathers Inn in Church Row, which were demolished in 1894 to improve both the view and access to the church.

Right: St Cuthbert's church in Darlington is one of the most important churches (architecturally) in the north of England. Building commenced at the end of the twelfth century on the orders of Bishop Pudsey (le Puiset) of Durham and the church was probably completed by 1240. The spire was added at the beginning of the fourteenth century.

Below: St Cuthbert's churchyard, c. 1890, crowded with tombstones. Unfortunately many interesting tombstones were removed and lost when the churchyard was landscaped to serve as one of the town's open spaces in 1970.

The funeral procession of Sir Edward Daniel Walker, three times mayor of the town and known as the 'Grand Old Man of Darlington', makes its way up the path of St Cuthbert's church in May 1919.

These buildings were demolished to make way for the new town hall. The Clarence Commercial Hotel, on the left, occupied the remnants of Feethams, a Pease house after which the street is named. On the right is the building which was used as the parcels office of the United Bus Company.

This early photograph (c. 1855) shows some of the shops in Tubwell Row. On the left at No. 7 was the premises of Mary Storrow who advertised herself as a 'Plumber, Turner, Glazier and Gas Fitter'. At No. 8 was Francis Hutchinson, a wireworker; at No. 9, Joseph Thornton and Peter Kemp Bailey, drapers and silk mercers; on the right at No. 10, William Hildreth, saddler.

Although this photograph was taken as recently as October 1987, it shows a Darlington scene which no longer exists. Taken from the rear of the Queen's Head in Tubwell Row and looking towards Priestgate, it shows a whole range of buildings (including part of the Darlington Co-operative Society building, surmounted by a cupola) which have since been demolished to make way for the Cornmill development. The area behind the low wall formed part of Penny Yard.

Tubwell Row, October 1987, showing the Raby Hotel, sandwiched between the mid-1960s buildings of the North Eastern Co-operative Society, all of them empty and awaiting demolition. The Darlington Co-operative Industrial and Provident Society first opened a store in Priestgate in 1868 and gradually expanded to occupy premises on both sides of that street. With its closure in 1986, before demolition to clear the site for the Cornmill development, the Co-op brought to an end its town centre presence which had lasted for 118 years.

THE DARLINGTON EQUITABLE
BUILDING SOCIETY.

(The Oldest society in the District. Established 1856.)

OFFICES :

Church Row, Market Place, DARLINGTON.

OPEN SATURDAYS. 9 to 1 ; OTHER DAYS, 9 to 6.

RESERVE FUND.		£	s.	d.
30th June, 1913		10,559	1	8
Added during year		732	16	4
30th June, 1914.		**£11,291**	**18**	**0**

Perfect Safety for Investors and Exceptional Advantages for Borrowers.

Interest Allowed to Ordinary Shareholders, 4 per cent.

Do.	do.	Realised	do.	$3\frac{1}{2}$	,,
Do.	do.	Depositors	-	$3\frac{1}{4}$	,,

DEPOSITS of £500 and upwards, at 6 months' notice, are allowed 4 per cent., payable half-yearly.

Investments receive full interest from Date of Receipt,
Advances on Eligible Property at $4\frac{1}{2}$ per cent. interest.

Full particulars and details on application to

ROBERT BYERS, SECRETARY.

Ask for Copy of Rules and last Balance Sheet.

The offices in Church Row (now mainly occupied by the Darlington Council for Voluntary Services) were built in 1902 for the Darlington Equitable Building Society which had been founded in 1856. Until 1890 when it moved to High Row the society had its offices in the Central Hall in Bull Wynd. In 1946 the DEBS amalgamated with the Durham & Yorkshire Building Society to form the Darlington Building Society, which moved to new offices in Tubwell Row in 1965.

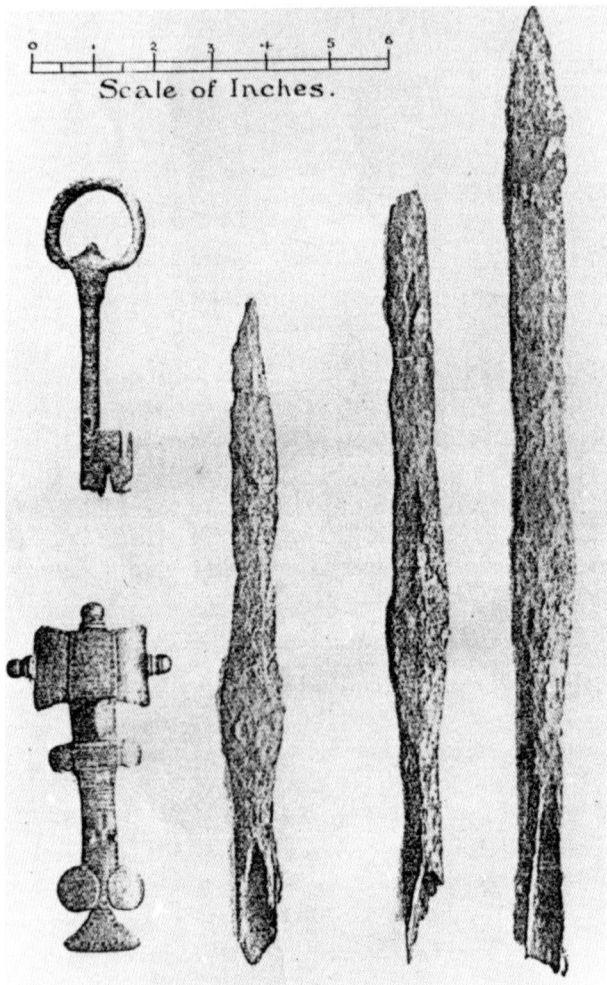

Scale of Inches.

In 1876 workmen excavating trenches for drains in Dodds Street uncovered a number of graves containing six skeletons and a quantity of grave goods, which were identified as belonging to the sixth or seventh century. Some came into the possession of J.T. Abbott, chemist, and were later sold to distant museums. Others were presented to the Darlington Museum in 1922. They include an iron key, a bronze brooch and spear heads. The site is believed to have been the cemetery for the town's Anglo-Saxon settlement.

DARLINGTON
PUBLIC MUSEUM
—
THE
PEARSON
COLLECTION
VIEW FROM THE
WEST END OF
ROOM

PHOTO HARROW

The Pearson collection of big game trophies was acquired by the Darlington Museum in 1921. Sydney James Pearson of Aysgarth, a keen field sportsman, went on an Arctic expedition and the first of many hunting trips to Africa in 1909. After his death in 1920 his family loaned, and later donated, his collection to the museum. By the end of the 1960s many of the exhibits were in poor condition and the collection was removed from display. On the closure of the Museum in 1998, its collections were dispersed. The building it occupied in Tubwell Row is now a drop-in centre for the charity, First Stop.

The photographer braved the heights of St Cuthbert's church tower to take this view, dominated by the chimney of Pease's Mill across the rooftops of Stone Bridge and Crown Street in the 1920s. Opposite the mill stands the printing works of Dressers and, on the opposite corner of Priestgate, the buildings of The Northern Echo, later to be extended further up Priestgate. On the skyline can be seen two church spires, that of the Union Street Congregational church on the left, while that of St George's Presbyterian church is on the right.

This aerial photograph of 1950 shows the extent of the Pease Mills which stood on both sides of the lower part of Priestgate. The site of the offices and spinning mill on the south side is now occupied by a branch of T K Max and a multi-storey car park. The weaving sheds on the north side were replaced in the 1960s by a bowling alley (since converted into a large retail unit and—a now defunct—nightclub). Most of the jumble of buildings in the yards between Priestgate and Tubell Row disappeared when the Cornmill Centre was built.

Left: Looking west along Priestgate in 1965, showing the Co-operative Society shops which lined the northern side of the street. These were subsequently demolished to make way for an extension and new entrance to the King's Head and a small row of shops, which have in turn been demolished to accommodate part of the Cornmill development.

Below: Before the coming of heavy industry Darlington's prosperity was based mainly on its market and the manufacture of textiles. This photograph shows one of Darlington's mills, which once stood on the mill race, in the course of demolition. The mill race ran from the Skerne at Russell Street beneath what is now East Street, behind the site of the public library, and rejoined the river close to the Stone Bridge.

The inscription on the Crown Street façade of this building proclaims it to be the 'E⁰ Pease Free Library 1884'. All attempts by a few farsighted individuals to persuade the town's ratepayers of the benefits of a public library had failed until Edward Pease, a grandson of the 'Father of Railways', died in 1880 and bequeathed £10,000 specifically for the purpose. His daughter, Lady Lymington, opened the building on 23 October 1885.

In March 1933 the library extension was opened. The new lending library had a large central circulation desk with gates to control the flow of borrowers. In January 1969 this desk and its large glass screen were removed, to be replaced by separate issue and discharge counters.

From its opening day in 1885, the reading room proved to be a very popular department of the library, open for 13 hours on each weekday and subscribing to 140 papers and magazines. In 1990 the reading room facilities were transferred to the reference library, and the reading room was converted into the Centre for Local Studies.

A·D· Coronation·1911
FIRST U·K·AERIAL POST
By Sanction of H·M·Postmaster General

(Address only to be written here.

S. Gosling Esq.,
    North Star,
        Darlington.

For Conveyance by AEROPLANE from LONDON
to WINDSOR. No responsibility in respect
of loss, damage, or delay, is undertaken
by the Postmaster General

S. Gosling, manager of the North Star newspaper, was the recipient of this postcard in 1911. Posted on 9 September by the Remington Typewriter Company as an advertisement for its products, it proudly proclaimed that it was the 'first postal message by aeroplane post' in the United Kingdom, the service flying between Hendon and Windsor. The North Star offices were housed in the building designed by G.G. Hoskins on the corner of Crown Street and Quebec Street.

DARLINGTON GARAGE,
LIMITED.

THE MOST COMMODIOUS.
THE MOST COMPLETE.

BODY BUILDING.
REPAIRS OF ALL DESCRIPTIONS
COACH PAINTING.   TRIMMING

Tel. 2304.   Telegrams : "GARAGE."

CROWN STREET (Near G.P.O.)

The Darlington Garage Limited had extensive premises in a street which has changed its name over the years, being originally Mill Street, then Crown Street and finally East Street. The garage was situated between the River Skerne and the town's registry office, roughly on the present site of the access road to the multi-storey car park and the rear of Marks & Spencer.

The Stone Bridge

This pen and ink drawing of the old Stone Bridge came from the skilled hand of Alfred Dresser in 1889. The pronounced hump of the bridge prevented the provision of a horse tram service to the part of the town on the east side of the Skerne. Although replaced by a cast-iron structure in 1895 the bridge still rejoices in the name of the Stone Bridge, and gives its name to the row of buildings which runs to the corner of Crown Street.

This postcard is one of a series issued to commemorate the unveiling of the South African War Memorial on St Cuthbert's Green by Field Marshal Lord Roberts in August 1905. Lord Roberts, in full dress uniform, can be seen passing through the gate of the green. The Darlington section of the county police force is much in evidence, its constables carrying folded capes in case of rain.

Parkgate led directly to the east end of the Stone Bridge. In this view, photographed around 1900, T. Reed, draper and milliner, displays his wares both within and without. The gas lamp was of a type used only at important road junctions, in this case that of Parkgate, Stone Bridge and Clay Row.

Darlington Corporation's Fire Brigade escape ladder No. 4 stands in pristine condition in the yard to the rear of the fire station in Borough Road. The appliance carries two extinguishers on the vertical stanchions, as well as a warning bell on the side of the vehicle.

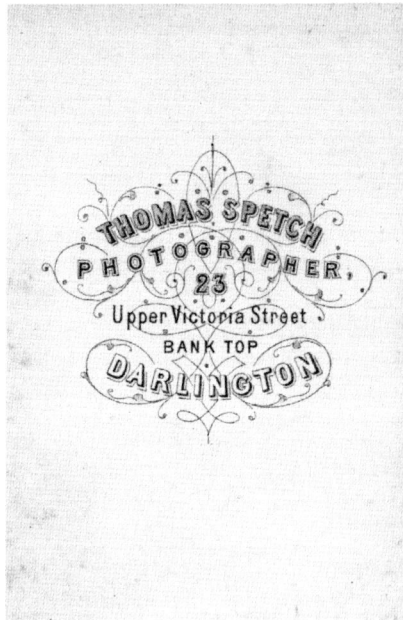

A carte-de-visite photograph (actual size) by Thomas Spetch, one of the town's many professional photographers. Mr Spetch, who described himself in the late 1870s as a 'bird and animal preserver and photographer', operated his business from his home in Upper Victoria Street. This ran from Neasham Road to Pattison Street and now forms part of Eastbourne Road. The identity of the lady is unknown.

The firm of Patons and Baldwins concentrated its activities in Darlington, opening its factory, the administration block of which is shown here, in December 1947. At the time it was the largest factory in the world devoted to the manufacture of hand-knitting yarns and yarns for the hosiery trade. In 1961 the company merged with that of J. & P. Coats and in the 1970s a considerable portion of the Darlington site was leased to the tobacco manufacturer Carreras Rothman, who started a production line in 1976. Following th closure of Carreras Rothmans in June 2004, much of the site has been redeveloped as the Lingfield Point Business Park.

Neasham Road, c. 1900. Once just the country lane to Neasham, this area of the town developed after the construction of Bank Top railway station. Many of the houses were occupied by railwaymen and their families, because of their close proximity to the station, goods depot and engine shed.

The vicarage of St John the Evangelist stood next to the church in Neasham Road. Although the parish was founded in 1845 the church did not open until January 1850, largely financed by the shareholders of the York, Newcastle and Berwick Railway Company, whose chairman George Hudson laid the foundation stone. An Anchor sheltered housing complex now stands on the site of the vicarage.

This photograph was taken from the roof of the Darlington Railway Plant and Foundry Company in Rocket Street, looking over the rooftops towards Yarm Road and the tower of the Corporation Welfare Establishment (East Haven) which, despite many official attempts to disguise its origins, was often referred to as 'the workhouse'.

Another photograph from the vantage point of the Railway Plant Works roof, looking across the rooftops to (on the right) Bank Top railway station and (on the left) the large sheds of the Cleveland Bridge and Engineering Company in Smithfield Road. In the foreground are Ethel, Stanley and Carlton Streets.

Yet another photograph from the same vantage point, c. 1950, showing Hundens Lane with its hospital and Eastbourne School beyond. The Municipal Isolation Hospital opened in 1874 to deal with cases of tuberculois, diphtheria, scarlet fever and other infectious diseases. Its name was changed later to the Darlington Infectious Diseases Hospital. With the decline in the occurrence of notifiable infectious diseases, the building served as an outpost of the Memorial Hospital, housing the ENT and Orthodontic Departments. In 1979 the unit closed and the buildings were demolished in 1982

.This building in Victoria Road housed the children's hospital, which was founded in 1869 and maintained at the expense of Miss Emma Gurney Pease, a daughter of Joseph Pease. At any one time it provided free accommodation and treatment for seven children who were often given free clothing on their discharge. The hospital closed in 1896, the year after Miss Pease's death, but was replaced by a children's ward at Greenbank Hospital, financed by a bequest from Miss Pease.

The view c. 1893 across the massed ranks of houses and smoking chimneys of Backhouse Street, Park Street, Park Place, Swan Street and Model Place to the town clock, Backhouse's Bank and St Cuthbert's. The chimney (centre left) belonged to the foundry of G. Denham, who manufactured many of the town's street grids.

The craftsmen and apprentices at the works of Edgar Cox-Walker in Houndgate in the 1940s. This electrical engineering works, founded in 1880, stood on the corner of Feethams and Houndgate. A pioneer of telephony, Edgar Cox-Walker installed a private telephone system for Darlington Corporation in 1881, only five years after Alexander Graham Bell patented the telephone.

North Eastern Hotel, Victoria Road, Darlington

Above: A cab horse plods its weary way up the steep incline of Victoria Road to the main entrance of Bank Top railway station. The buildings on the left were occupied by Joseph John Thompson, fruit merchant; the North Bitchburn Coal Company; Percy Wood; Robert Wood, coal merchant; and the North Eastern Hotel.

Left: The North Eastern Hotel (now the Coachman) was built in the early 1880s to cater for travellers using the services of the North Eastern Railway. The hotel had stabling for thirty horses, and a large coach house in which the carriages of patrons could be housed.

Seven

Leisure

This avenue of trees once formed part of the eastern edge of the Southend estate of Joseph Pease. After his death his two unmarried daughters continued to live there. In 1897 the estate was sold for housing development but this narrow strip with its avenue of trees was retained for public use as a 'pleasure ground', and was officially opened by the mayor on 1 January 1901.

The Grotto in South Park is now a grass plot shaded by trees. Originally it had a small pond with an island in the centre and was a tranquil spot from which to listen to the music from the nearby bandstand.

Opposite above: The Park House in South Park, with its Tudor-style chimneys, was built in the 1850s to provide accommodation for the park-keeper. In 1901 the height of its tower was increased to accommodate a clock which had been presented to the town. On the grass slope beneath the terrace can be seen a good floral representation of Darlington's first shield of arms.

Opposite below: Poor Howdens, the land on which the original part of South Park was laid out, formed part of a charity endowment administered by the Select Vestry, the 'Four and Twenty', of St Cuthbert's church. The planting of the park was carried out largely at the expense of Joseph Pease. In 1877 the town corporation purchased the twenty acres, previously rented from the charity trustees, and gradually extended the area of the park to its present total of ninety-two acres.

Alderman Crooks, a well known character in the town, was often the target of the *Northern Despatch* cartoonist, 'Pip'. Tommy Crooks, a keen cyclist, was usually depicted carrying an umbrella and wearing bicycle clips. This particular cartoon alludes to the campaign to create an open-air swimming pool in South Park. The idea came to nothing. Instead the Gladstone Baths, adjoining the town's original baths in Kendrew Street, were built with a common entrance in Gladstone Street.

Darlingtonians had to wait until 1902 for municipal bowling greens in South Park. The town's bowls players made representations to the council after visiting the municipal greens in South Shields.

Darlington is to be congratulated on the number of parks and open spaces within the town. The opening of the seven-acre Eastbourne Park, created on land bought for £1,000 from the trustees of the Middleton estate in May 1902, brought the number of municipally owned recreation grounds at that time to seven.

The Darlington Saxhorn Band, founded by George Hoggett, had a national reputation, coming fourth in a competition at the Crystal Palace in 1859 and winning first prize in a contest at Newcastle. After George's death in 1876 the band was led by Henry Hoggett, another member of this talented musical family. The Saxhorn Band was later absorbed into the band of the Darlington Volunteers.

As can be seen from this advertisement of 1903, the Bridge Hotel and the adjacent Theatre Royal (now the Odeon Cinema) were managed as one company. Its managing director, Mr Jennings, seems to have considered it necessary to defend himself against the onslaughts of both unscrupulous tradesmen and 'disorderly persons'.

Cyril Maude (1862–1951) was born in London. After emigrating to Canada he made his stage début in Denver, Colorado. On his return to London in 1885, he established himself as an actor/manager and, after further visits to America and Australia, formed his own touring company in 1919. This postcard was produced for sale to Darlington's theatre-goers.

"THE BELLE OF NEW YORK."

MAUD DARLING
as
"THE BELLE OF NEW YORK."
Tuesday, Thursday and Saturday.

THEATRE ROYAL,
DARLINGTON,
Monday, November 4th, 1901.

RETURN VISIT OF

The Ben Greet No. 1 Co.

IN

The Belle of
New York

Portrait Souvenir of

MISS MAUD DARLING

AS

"THE BELLE OF NEW YORK."

AND

"FIFI,"

which characters she will sustain on alternate
nights throughout the week.

William Watson, saddler, carried on his business in the shop at the corner of Prebend Row and
Tubwell Row. His daughter Maud, who was born in 1881, became a star of musical comedy and
light opera under the name of Maud Darling, an obvious allusion to her home town. She died
of tuberculosis in 1927. A large studio portrait of Maud Darling, from the camera of Sydney H.
Wood, was presented to the Civic Theatre by her great-nephew in 1968.

A 1937 production of *Robin Hood and His Merry Men*, performed in the church hall by the pupils of St Mary's C. of E. School, Cockerton.

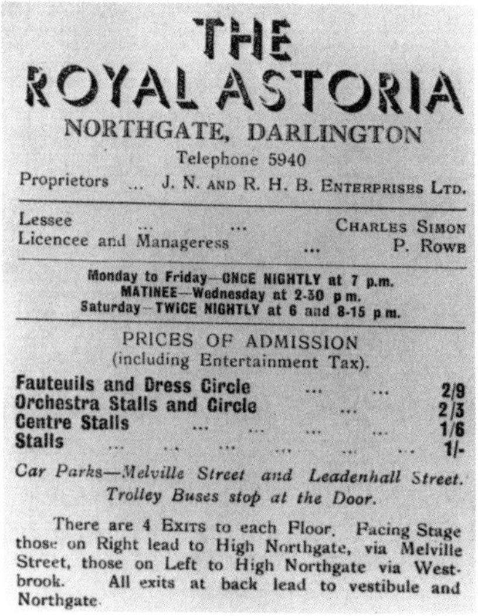

THE
ROYAL ASTORIA
NORTHGATE, DARLINGTON
Telephone 5940

Proprietors ... J. N. AND R. H. B. ENTERPRISES LTD.

Lessee ... ... CHARLES SIMON
Licencee and Manageress ... P. ROWE

Monday to Friday—ONCE NIGHTLY at 7 p.m.
MATINEE—Wednesday at 2-30 p.m.
Saturday—TWICE NIGHTLY at 6 and 8-15 p.m.

PRICES OF ADMISSION
(including Entertainment Tax).

Fauteuils and Dress Circle	2/9
Orchestra Stalls and Circle	2/3
Centre Stalls	1/6
Stalls	1/-

Car Parks—Melville Street and Leadenhall Street.
Trolley Buses stop at the Door.

There are 4 EXITS to each Floor. Facing Stage those on Right lead to High Northgate, via Melville Street, those on Left to High Northgate via Westbrook. All exits at back lead to vestibule and Northgate.

The Royal Astoria, Northgate occupied Livingstone Hall, whose main entrance was in High Northgate opposite John Street. The hall, which had been built in 1873, had been the venue for a variety of events and entertainments, Salvation Army services, roller-skating, music hall, cinema and theatre. At the time of this 1949 advertisement it had become the home of the Darlington Repertory Company. After its closure in September 1958, Livingstone Hall was demolished.

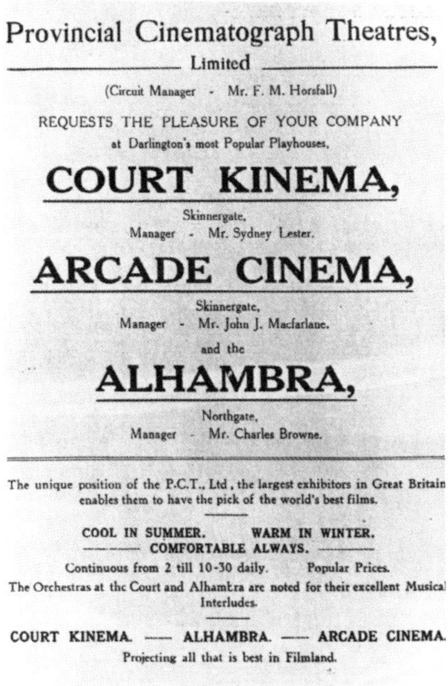

Provincial Cinematograph Theatres,
Limited
(Circuit Manager - Mr. F. M. Horsfall)

REQUESTS THE PLEASURE OF YOUR COMPANY
at Darlington's most Popular Playhouses,

COURT KINEMA,
Skinnergate,
Manager - Mr. Sydney Lester.

ARCADE CINEMA,
Skinnergate,
Manager - Mr. John J. Macfarlane.
and the

ALHAMBRA,
Northgate,
Manager - Mr. Charles Browne.

The unique position of the P.C.T., Ltd , the largest exhibitors in Great Britain enables them to have the pick of the world's best films.

COOL IN SUMMER. WARM IN WINTER.
COMFORTABLE ALWAYS.
Continuous from 2 till 10-30 daily. Popular Prices.
The Orchestras at the Court and Alhambra are noted for their excellent Musical Interludes.

COURT KINEMA. —— ALHAMBRA. —— ARCADE CINEMA.
Projecting all that is best in Filmland.

A 1925 advertisement for three of Darlington's cinemas. The sites of the Alhambra, Northgate and the Arcade, Skinnergate are now covered by Northgate House and the Gala Bingo Club respectively. The façade of the Court Kinema (later the Court Arcade) can still be seen above Nos. 8 and 9 Skinnergate.

In 1920 the Royal Agricultural Society of England Show was held in Darlington. From 29 June to 3 July, despite indifferent weather, almost 133,000 people, including the Duke of York (later George VI), attended the showground at Hundens Farm, breaking all previous attendance records. To coincide with the show an evening entertainment in South Park was organized, at which collections were taken for the hospital building fund. This postcard was printed specially to advertise the stand of one of the show's exhibitors.

If White Bros of Northgate offered a motor-cycle combination for sale at £82 to the modern-day equivalent of the Pip family, the queue would stretch from High Row to the showrooms. The company still trades from the same address on the corner of Northgate and Corporation Road but the makes of machine offered for sale are very different from those available in 1929.

Eight

Public Transport

RAPID, SAFE, AND CHEAP TRAVELLING
By the Elegant NEW RAILWAY COACH,

THE UNION,

*Which will COMMENCE RUNNING on the STOCKTON and DARLINGTON RAILWAY, on MONDAY
the 16th day of October, 1826,*

And will call at Yarm, and pass within a mile of Middleton Spa, on its way from Stockton to Darlington, and *vice versa.*

FARES.   Inside 1½d.—Outside, 1d. per Mile.   Parcels in proportion.

No gratuities expected by the Guard or Coachman.

N. B. The Proprietors will not be accountable for any Parcel of more than £5. value, unless entered and paid for accordingly.

The UNION will run from the Black Lion Hotel and New Inn, Stockton, to the New Inn, Yarm, and to the Black Swan Inn, near the Croft Branch, Darlington; at each of which Inns passengers and parcels are booked, and the times of starting may be ascertained, as also at the Union Inn, Yarm, and Talbot Inn, Darlington.

On the 19th and 20th of October, the Fair Days at Yarm, the Union will leave Darlington at six in the morning for Yarm, and will leave Yarm for Darlington again at six in the evening; in the intermediate time, each day, it will ply constantly between Stockton and Yarm, leaving each place every half hour.

(From the *Durham County Advertiser,* 14th October, 1826.)

The Stockton and Darlington Railway (S&DR), built to carry coal and minerals, opened on 27 September 1825. Immediately there was a demand to provide a passenger service and the company permitted privately owned coaches, such as The Union, to use the line between Darlington and Stockton. Prospective passengers from Darlington were advised to enquire about departure times at the Talbot Inn, which stood on the corner of High Row and Post House Wynd, or at the Black Swan in Parkgate, from where the coach departed.

STOCKTON & DARLINGTON RAILWAY COACHES.

The **SUMMER ARRANGEMENTS** will cease on the 30th Instant, and the Trains run the same as last season until further notice: *viz.—*

Winter Arrangements, commencing October 1st, 1840.

ST. HELEN'S AUCKLAND TO DARLINGTON.		DARLINGTON TO ST. HELEN'S AUCKLAND.	
First Trip	at half-past Eight o'Clock.	First Trip	at half-past Eight o'Clock.
Second Trip	at One "	Second Trip	at One "
Third Trip	at Five "	Third Trip	at Five "

DARLINGTON TO STOCKTON.		STOCKTON TO DARLINGTON.	
Merchandize Train	at half-past Six o'Clock.	First Class Train	at 10 min. bef. Eight o'Clock.
First Class Train	at half-past Nine "	Merchandize Train at 10 min. bef. Nine "	
Merchandize Train	at Eleven "	First Class Train	at 20 min. past Twelve "
First Class Train	at Two "	Merchandize Train at 20 min. past Two "	
Merchandize Train	at Four "	First Class Train	at 20 min. past Four "
First Class Train	at Six "	Merchandize Train at 20 min. past Six "	

STOCKTON TO MIDDLESBRO'.		MIDDLESBRO' TO STOCKTON	
First Trip	at Eight o'Clock.	*First Trip	at half-past Seven o'Clock.
Second do	at Nine "	Second do	at half-past Eight "
*Third do	at Ten "	Third do	at half-past Nine "
Fourth do	at Eleven "	Fourth do	at half-past Ten "
Fifth do	at half-past Twelve "	*Fifth do	at Twelve "
Sixth do	at half-past One "	Sixth do	at One "
*Seventh do	at half-past Two "	Seventh do	at Two "
Eighth do	at half-past Three "	Eighth do	at Three "
Ninth do	at half-past Four "	*Ninth do	at Four "
Tenth do	at half-past Five "	Tenth do	at Five "
*Eleventh do	at a quarter bef. Seven "	Eleventh do	at Six "

* Are in connexion with the first class Trains to and from Darlington.

Tickets must be taken at least Five Minutes before the Trains start.

NO SMOKING ALLOWED IN ANY OF THE COMPANY'S COACHES.

MARKET COACHES.

A Coach and Cattle Carriage will leave St. Helen's Auckland, on Mondays, at half-past Six o'Clock; and Shildon, at Seven in the Morning.

HORSES, CATTLE, AND CARRIAGES, CAREFULLY CONVEYED BETWEEN STOCKTON AND DARLINGTON, BY THE MERCHANDIZE TRAINS:

Horse, 2s.—Gig, 2s. or Horse and Gig, 3s.—Four-wheeled Carriage, 5s., or with Two Horses, 8s.—Horned Cattle, 1s. 6d. each:—Sheep, 4d. each, or 5s. per Score.—Dogs, 1s. each:

If by the FIRST-CLASS Train ; Horse 3s.—Gig, 3s.—Horse and Gig, 4s.—Four-wheeled Carriage, 5s., or with Two Horses, 9s.

Railway Office, Darlington, September 25th, 1840.

COATES AND FARMER, PRINTERS, HIGH ROW, DARLINGTON.

The S&DR very quickly realized the advantages of poster advertising and the potential market for the speedy transport of livestock.

RAILWAY COMMUNICATION

BETWEEN

LONDON,

Darlington, and Newcastle.

IMPORTANT

INFORMATION

To TRAVELLERS.

The Public are respectfully informed that, on and after *Thursday, the 5th of May* next, an expeditious, commodious, and economical Communication will be opened from the GREAT NORTH OF ENGLAND RAILWAY STATION at DARLINGTON, to *Durham, Shields, Sunderland,* and *Newcastle.*

The Route will be by the STOCKTON and DARLINGTON RAILWAY to SOUTH CHURCH, near Bishop Auckland, thence by well-appointed Omnibuses, and the DURHAM JUNCTION and BRANDLING JUNCTION RAILWAYS, in connection with Trains to and from Dinsdale Baths, Yarm, Stockton, and Middlesbrough.

The Trains will start from each end Four times a day, and the distance be performed in about 3 hours and a quarter.

From DARLINGTON.	From GATESHEAD, SUNDERLAND and SHIELDS.
7·0 a.m.	8·0 a.m.
10·0 „	11·0 „
2·0 p.m.	2·0 p.m.
5·30 „	6·0 „

FARES:

From Darlington throughout to Gateshead, Sunderland, and Shields.

1st Class, 8s. | 2nd Class, 6s.

April 22nd, 1842

In 1841 the Great North of England Railway Company authorized the completion of the route from Darlington to Gateshead, using a line due north from Bank Top, despite strong representations from the S&DR that the route should run via its tracks. In 1842, in an attempt to poach passengers, the S&DR advertised a service via North Road station and Shildon to South Church, from where the unfortunate travellers were conveyed by road to Rainton, near Houghton-le-Spring, where they again boarded a train. Not surprisingly this service was not a success.

In 1875 the North Eastern Railway Company and the Corporation of Darlington joined forces to provide a programme of events to celebrate the fiftieth anniversary of the opening of the S&DR. At the exhibition of locomotives in North Road Works, pride of place was given to *Locomotion*, the engine which had pulled the first train on 27 September 1825. It was estimated that 50,000 people had attended during the two days of the exhibition.

The 1875 celebrations were the brainchild of Henry Pease of Pierremont, a son of Edward Pease, the 'Father of Railways', and the vice-chairman of the North Eastern Railway Company. To him fell the task of overseeing the arrangements of the events, one of which was a banquet held in a marquee on Feethams cricket field.

In 1854 John Dixon, the Engineer to the S&DR, suggested that the company's locomotive works at Shildon should be resited. Three years later the decision was taken to build at Darlington, and on 1 January 1863 the North Road Works of the S&DR were opened. Six months later the S&DR amalgamated with the North Eastern Railway Company. This plan shows the extent of the works around 1910, when its manager was N.J. Lockyer.

One of the most important officers in any railway company was the Chief Mechanical Engineer. Vincent L. Raven, the CME of the North Eastern Railway, and his staff moved into Stooperdale Offices, Brinkburn Road (shown here in an architect's drawing) in April 1912. The fountain in front of the *porte-cochère* was never installed.

In the early hours of 15 November 1910, a freight train from Newcastle ploughed into the rear of a stationary goods train on the through line just outside Darlington Bank Top station, strewing wreckage across all four lines. Both the driver and fireman of the freight train were killed.

At about 11.15 p.m. on 27 June 1928, a terrible train disaster occurred at the south end of Bank Top station. An excursion train returning from Scarborough to Newcastle collided with a shunting engine. Of the twenty-five people killed, fourteen were members of a women's organization from Hetton-le-Hole. The injured were treated at Greenbank Hospital.

JIMMY JAMES.

THE ENTIRE PROCEEDS FROM THE SALE OF THESE PHOTOGRAPHS WILL BE
DEVOTED TO THE ORPHANS AND DEPENDANTS OF THOSE KILLED & INJURED IN

THE DARLINGTON TRAIN DISASTER, JUNE 27th 1928.

25 Lives Lost   About 50 Injured.

After the disaster many fund-raising events were held to assist the bereaved
and injured. The popular music hall comedian, Jimmy James, donated all
the proceeds from the sale of this postcard to the disaster fund. Born in
Stockton in 1892, Jimmy James, whose real name was James Casey, was
renowned as a master of timing and ad libbing. After his death in 1965 his
son, Jimmy Casey, carried on his father's act.

Although it is generally recognized that Edward Pease was the driving force behind the establishment of the S&DR, his part in the formation of the company of Robert Stephenson, engine builders of Newcastle, is often overlooked. This resolution, dated 8 July 1823 and bearing the signatures of the four partners in the enterprise, George Stephenson, his son Robert, Edward Pease and Michael Longridge, records the decision to purchase the site of the original engine works in Newcastle.

Above: The firm of Robert Stephenson, which built the No. 1 engine, *Locomotion*, for the S&DR, moved from Newcastle to Darlington in 1900. In the 1920s, it received a commission to construct a replica of the famous engine Rocket, which had been built by the company in 1829. The original *Rocket* had taken part in the Rainhill Trials, organized by the Liverpool and Manchester Railway Company to determine the most efficient type of steam locomotive, and had won a prize of £500.

Right: In 1935 the curator of the Science Museum in London, in which the original *Rocket* was displayed, commissioned Robert Stephenson & Hawthorn Ltd to build another replica, shown here in the course of construction at the company's Springfield, Darlington works.

To celebrate the centenary of the opening of the S&DR, the London and North Eastern Railway Company (LNER) decided to stage a procession of locomotives from Stockton to Darlington, headed by *Locomotion*. The second engine in the procession was *Derwent* (pictured here) which had been built in 1845 to the design of Timothy Hackworth in the Hopetown Foundry, owned by William and Alfred Kitching. Both *Locomotion* and *Derwent* can now be seen in the Darlington Railway Museum.

As part of the three-day celebrations of the S&DR centenary, the LNER also staged an exhibition in the newly built wagon works at Faverdale. The exhibition was officially opened by the Duke of York (later George VI), accompanied by the duchess. The locomotives which had taken part in the procession were lined up for visitors to inspect. No. 12 was an LNER Doncaster-built 'Mikado' type, No. 25 a North British 'Atlantic'.

Under both the LNER and British Railways, Darlington was an important steam locomotive depot. This interesting edifice, the coaling plant by which engines were refuelled (built in 1939), was demolished in December 1967.

A double-headed British Railways train leaves Darlington North Road station on its way to Bank Top. After years of neglect North Road station gained a new lease of life in 1975, when the station buildings and the left-hand side of the platform in this photograph became the town's railway museum. Trains to and from Bishop Auckland still use the right-hand platform.

A faked 'meeting' of two famous railway locomotives. A photograph of *Locomotion* has been superimposed on a 1925 shot of the *Flying Scotsman* approaching Darlington from the north.

The 1844 Newcastle and Darlington Junction Railway crossed the 1825 route of the S&DR at right angles, east of North Road station. The crossing was controlled from its own signal box (since demolished). The S&DR lines have been removed and the site marked with an explanatory sign.

DARLINGTON
STREET RAILROAD COMPANY
(LIMITED.)

NOTICE!

In order to accommodate Parties travelling by the Street Cars. Tickets will be issued in quantities on the following terms, viz :—

100 Tickets	(which at usual fares would be 16s. 8d.)		for	**14s. 0d.**
50 „	(„	„	8s. 4d.) „	**7s. 0d.**
25 „	(„	„	4s. 2d.) „	**3s. 6d.**

These are sold at the Company's Office; and may also be had of Mr C W. Hird, Railway Station, Darlington; Mr. G. Simpson, High Row; Mr. B..son

Darlington, an early pioneer in public road transport, had the third horse-drawn tramway system in the country. It opened in January 1862 and ran between Prebend Row and North Road station. The street railroad did not prosper and the lines were removed in 1864.

In October 1880 a horse tram service again started operating in the town, running along Woodland Road to the outskirts of Cockerton, up North Road as far as Westmoreland Street and (for a very short period) to Bank Top station via Victoria Road. Here double-decker car No. 53, with a very youthful conductor and a driver not yet supplied with a uniform waits in North Road.

Car Driven by the Mayoress (Mrs. Henderson).

Right: On 18 August 1903 the horse tram service ceased, to be replaced by the electric Darlington Corporation Light Railway which opened on 1 June 1904. To commemorate the event, *The Northern Echo* issued a series of postcards, of which this is one. The first tramcar was driven by Mrs Henderson, the mayoress and wife of Arthur Henderson, mayor of Darlington and MP for Barnard Castle. Mrs Wilkes was the wife of Alderman J.J. Wilkes, chairman of the municipal Electric Lighting and Tramways Committee.

Below: The electric tram routes ran to Cockerton and Harrowgate Hill, along Haughton Road as far as Barton Street and along Yarm Road as far as Cobden Street. Here tramcar No. 2, with its crew and an inspector resplendent in their new uniforms, stands in Yarm Road which was then little more than a country lane.

Car Driven by Mrs. Wilkes.

Northern Echo Snapshots.

Between January and April 1926 the electric tram service was itself replaced by trolley buses, or 'trackless trams' as they were originally called. Three of the four existing routes were extended to serve the expanding suburbia of Haughton, Faverdale and Geneva Road. Here bus No. 11 (with solid tyres) waits in Prebend Row.

Darlington Corporation was justly proud of its trolley bus fleet and took pains to record for posterity the delivery of new vehicles. It is doubtful whether the electricity supply would have been able to cope with the running of these three buses, photographed in Haughton Road in 1929, so close to each other.

With the exception of the necessary overhead wiring and its supporting stanchions which spoiled the skyline and cluttered the pavement, trolley buses could be said to have been environmentally friendly, non-polluting and silent. For a short period, double-deck trolley buses were to be seen in Darlington, the corporation taking delivery of six in 1949 which were used on the Park Lane to Faverdale and Cockerton to Coniscliffe Road routes. Low bridges in Parkgate, North Road and Haughton Road made it impossible to use double-deckers on the town's other routes and the decision was taken to sell them in 1952.

Gradually, between November 1951 and August 1957, the internal combustion engine ousted electricity on Darlington's public transport routes. This single-decker in the town's original blue livery turns the corner at the top of Tubwell Row, beneath the trolley bus wires.

A Daimler double-decker on the 6A route through Auckland Oval in the late 1970s. Auckland Oval forms part of the estate of 200 houses which was constructed in 1926 for employees of the London and North Eastern Railway Company by the building firm of J. Laing, the whole estate being completed in exactly eleven months. Many of the men who lived on the estate were employed at the newly built Faverdale Works.

Corporation bus No. 2 at Haughton Road Depot in the late 1970s. Built in 1964, it was approaching the end of its service to Darlington passengers, being withdrawn in 1980. Until the deregulation of road public transport in October 1986, under the 1985 Transport Act, Darlington Borough Transport had the exclusive right to provide a bus service within the town under the terms of a 'gentlemen's agreement' between it and the United Bus Company.

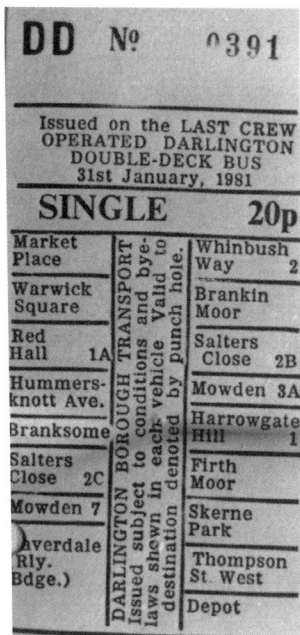

A collector's item for bus enthusiasts. One of the special tickets issued to mark the running of the last two man operated (driver and conductor) double-decker in the town.

A Daimler Roadliner on West Row in 1978. OMO (one man operated) buses had been introduced into Darlington in March 1967 but it was February 1981 before all routes were fully converted. The 'Autofare' system which dispensed with the giving of change was introduced on one route in 1974 and was speedily extended to all OMO services.

A Daimler OMO bus waiting at the Harrowgate Hill terminus of the No. 1 service before commencing its journey to Red Hall via the town centre. The small lay-by in which it stands formed part of the turning circle originally constructed for trolley buses.

The Darlington Triumph Services Ltd which was established in the early 1920s operated routes to Sunderland, Middlesbrough, Barnard Castle and even Blackpool. A subsidiary company, the Fawn Lea Omnibus Company, ran a service into Upper Teesdale. Most services carried both passengers and parcels. In 1950 the company was sold to the British Transport Commission and the majority of its routes were taken over by the Durham District Services Ltd. The company's office was in Horsemarket, in a building which was demolished to make way for the Dolphin Centre.

One of the Darlington Triumph Services' rural routes. In its early years many of its vehicles consisted of ex-War Department chassis surmounted by new bodywork.

In 1912 the United Automobile Services Ltd commenced operation in Lowestoft and Bishop Auckland. The company's headquarters were moved from York to Grange Road, Darlington in 1932. A Bristol Lodekka type double-decker was first purchased in 1955. This 1978 photograph shows one at the exit to the Feethams bus station, which was opened in September 1961 to replace the company's open waiting area in the Leadyard, just south of St Cuthbert's churchyard.

The staff of Kitching's Foundry. In 1790 William Kitching, a Darlington Quaker, opened an ironmonger's shop in Tubwell Row, with a small foundry behind. In 1824 the supplying of nails to the Stockton and Darlington Railway Company marked the start of its long involvement with the railway industry. In 1830 Kitching's Railway Foundry in Hopetown opened, and was soon producing locomotives. Eventually Kitching's was to form the nucleus of the Whessoe Foundry Company Ltd in Brinkburn Road.

Acknowledgements

I am most grateful to the following people who provided helpful information, loaned material and gave permission for its use in this book:

Mrs J. Chatt • Mr Gordon Coates • Mrs Duguid • Mr J.W. Fell
Mr Colin G. Flynn • The late Mr K. Hoole • Miss J.V. Redhead
Miss Audrey M. Reid • Mrs K. Singlehurst • Mr Edwin Smith
Mr Alan Suddes, Durham County Library

I am greatly indebted to those journalists and photographers of *The Northern Echo*, *Northern Despatch*, *Evening Despatch*, *Darlington and Stockton Times* and *North Star* who, over the years, have recorded the life of the town.
I should like to thank especially the staff of the Reference Library and Local Studies Centre of the Edward Pease Public Library for dealing with my endless queries and requests for material with unfailing patience and good humour.
I am especially grateful to my wife, Brenda, for her support, wealth of local knowledge and typing skills.